# The Pâtisseries of Paris

The

# PÂTISSERIES
## of PARIS

by
*Jamie Cahill*

PHOTOGRAPHS *by* ALISON HARRIS

### THE LITTLE BOOKROOM

NEW YORK

© 2007 The Little Bookroom
Text © 2007 Jamie Cahill
Photographs © 2007 Alison Harris

Book design: Louise Fili Ltd

Printed in China

Library of Congress Cataloging-in-Publication Data

Cahill, Jamie.
The patisseries of Paris : chocolatiers, tea salons, ice cream parlors, and
more / by Jamie Cahill; photographs by Alison Harris.
p. cm.
Includes index.
ISBN 1-892145-52-9 (alk. paper)
1.  Confectionery—France—Paris. 2.  Pastry--France—Paris. 3.
Desserts—France—Paris. 4.  Restaurants—France—Guidebooks.  I. Title.
TX793C34 2007
641.8'60944'361--dc22
[B]
2007020780

Published by The Little Bookroom
435 Hudson Street, 3rd Floor
New York NY 10014
editorial@littlebookroom.com
www.littlebookroom.com

10  9  8  7  6  5  4  3  2  1

Distributed in the U.S. by Random House, in the U.K. and Ireland by
Signature Book Services, and in Europe by Random House International.

For Tom, Lucie, and Emmett,

who ate many pastries to help me in my research

# CONTENTS

# INTRODUCTION

I'VE SPENT FOUR YEARS COMBING PARIS IN SEARCH OF THE BEST *PÂTISSERIES*, CHOCOLATE SHOPS, AND OTHER SPOTS TO SATISFY TRAVELERS WHO WANT TO EXPERIENCE THE CITY OF LIGHT BITE BY BITE. MOST SAVVY VISITORS HAVE DONE THEIR RESTAURANT RESEARCH AND HAVE PLANNED THEIR PRECIOUS FEW PARIS MEALS. BUT WHO POINTS THEM TO PARIS' BEST FLAN, *TARTE AUX FIGUES*, OR *FINANCIER*? THE BEST *PÂTISSERIES* CAN BE SURPRISINGLY DIFFICULT TO FIND.

With *The Pâtisseries of Paris* in hand, Francophiles and first-time visitors alike can score Parisians' favorite croissant, sample Louis XIV's beloved *baba au rhum* (still sold at Paris' oldest *pâtisserie*), or savor the city's most fancifully flavored *macarons*. In addition to almost 100 profiles of the city's best sweet spots, I've included other discoveries like the best time to land a table at Angelina, the legendary (and always crowded!) *salon de thé*; picturesque picnic spots; non-smoking café options; what time of day Parisians in the know get items as they come out of the oven; and more. To further whet your appetite, there's a profile of a chocolate buyer for the Fauchon gourmet store, a behind-the-scenes look at a day in a *pâtisserie* kitchen, the history of the *madeleine*, the éclair, and *tarte Tatin*; the difference between the dense richness of French *glace* and the creamy consistency of Italian *gelato*, and more. Now, on to the lemon tarts...the buttery *madeleines*... the oozing dark chocolate cake...or maybe a light-as-air *brioche*, slathered in jam...

Jamie Cahill

CITRON

0.80€

# FIRST
*Arrondissement*

# 215

215, RUE SAINT-HONORÉ, 1ST ARR.

*Telephone* ✦ 01 42 61 18 04

*Métro* ✦ TUILERIES

*Open* MONDAY *through* SATURDAY 7:30AM *to* 7:30PM ✦ *Closed* SUNDAY

AN OASIS IN THE FIRST ARRONDISSEMENT, WHERE GOOD *PÂT-ISSERIES* OR BOULANGERIES ARE IN SHORT SUPPLY, 215 sells some of the best fruit *clafoutis* (a cross between a pudding and a cake) I've tasted. Good to know, since in this neighborhood in between the Louvre and the shops of rue Saint-Honoré, visitors and locals alike are likely to find themselves needing a sugar boost. And, just one block up from the Tuileries, the location is convenient for buying a quick lunch to eat in the park.

Stick with the *tarte au citron* or *flan au chocolat* and skip the American-style cookies. The sandwiches, quiches, and other savories are all homemade.

Aside from the tasty sweets and lunch items, 215 has a few seats, a clean restroom, and sells bottles of water—surprisingly, not always an easy combination to find.

# Angelina

226, RUE DE RIVOLI, 1ST ARR.

Telephone ✦ 01 42 60 82 00

Métro ✦ TUILERIES

Open DAILY 8AM to 7PM

A NGELINA IS LEGENDARY FOR ITS HOT CHOCOLATE AND *MONT BLANC* PASTRY, BUT THE REAL APPEAL IS ITS BUSTLING vibe and elegant, Belle Epoque interior. Bask in the spacious "see and be seen" room of oversized, gold gilt mirrors, panels painted with pastoral scenes, and marble-topped tables—and be transported to enchanting, turn-of-the-last-century Paris.

The place is filled with tourists and locals alike, almost all relishing *le chocolat Africain*, hot chocolate so rich you practically need to eat it with a spoon. Those who aren't sipping it are cracking into the hard meringue of the *Mont Blanc* after conquering its outer mounds of whipped cream and squiggles of candied chestnut cream.

Angelina's extensive sweet selection, served all day, includes ice cream, chocolates, and all the favorite Parisian pastries. A full menu of salads, soups, quiches, or more complicated classic French fare is available at lunchtime. There is usually a line for a table, but people move in and out quickly, so the wait is rarely as long as it looks. Breakfast is the least busy time, with an eight to noon *petit déjeuner* special of coffee, tea, or hot chocolate with choice of *viennoiserie* or *tartine de pain à la ancienne* (crusty bread served with butter, honey, and homemade jams). If you are really hungry, you can also add fruit salad and your choice of eggs or smoked salmon.

# Aux Castelblangeois

168, RUE SAINT-HONORÉ, 1ST ARR.

*Telephone* ✦ 01 42 60 77 40

*Métro* ✦ LOUVRE-RIVOLI

*Open* MONDAY *through* FRIDAY 6:45AM *to* 8PM,
SATURDAY 7AM *to* 7:30PM ✦ *Closed* SUNDAY

AROUND THE CORNER FROM THE LOUVRE IN AN AREA LACK-
ING QUALITY *PÂTISSERIES*, AUX CASTELBLANGEOIS IS WORTH
a stop for its specialty, *l'elegance*, an appropriately-named,
white-chocolate-covered bundle of three varieties of chocolate mousse
and chocolate cake. The fruit cream desserts are unremarkable, but
in a pinch, the tarts, *viennoiserie*, and chocolate mousse are tasty. Aux
Castelblangeois also makes an excellent traditional baguette and good
savory options for a Louvre courtyard or Pont des Arts picnic.

# La Boulangerie Julien

75, RUE SAINT-HONORÉ, 1ST ARR.

Telephone ✦ 01 42 36 24 83

Métro ✦ LOUVRE-RIVOLI, PONT NEUF

Open MONDAY through SATURDAY 6:30AM to 8PM

THERE IS OFTEN A LINE OUTSIDE JULIEN: AT LUNCHTIME, WHEN THE SHOP DOES A BRISK BUSINESS OF QUICHES, *tourtes*, sandwiches, and salads to go, and in the evening, when its famous baguette *tradition* comes out of the oven.

Julien's sweet specialty is its *Jurassien,* an uncommon *sablé* cookie with crumble and fruit toppings such as apple cinnamon, pear chocolate, or raspberry orange, among others. Their buttery yet firm texture gives them a satisfying crunch. Unique Julien pastry creations include the *extrême* (vanilla *crème brulée* with dark chocolate mousse on an almond biscuit) and the *malicieux* (a molten chocolate cake topped with caramel *crème brulée*). Julien's tarts are hard to resist, with countless delicious choices like apricot, pear *Normande* or pear *amande* (with egg custard or almond flour fillings, respectively), rhubarb, or just plain apple. Wholesome wedges of flans are appealing, available in *nature* (plain), cherry, or coconut. Julien's secret lemon tart recipe is *"bien apprécié"* by clients.

Croissants are a hit, too. Julien sells about 1,300 each day, most before 10 a.m. During Fashion Week, business booms with orders from the likes of Yves St. Laurent and Louis Vuitton. They prefer the "mini" *viennoiserie*, bite-sized versions of all the buttery favorites, says *pâtissier* Stephane Varin.

If you are visiting Versailles, you can visit Julien at 60, rue de la Paroisse (01 39 50 01 84), located in a beautiful historic shop not far from the chateau.

### ✦ ✦ ✦ Additional Location ✦ ✦ ✦

85, RUE SAINT DOMINIQUE, 7TH ARR.

Telephone 01 45 51 88 77 ✦ Métro LA TOUR-MAUBOURG

Open MONDAY through SATURDAY 7:30PM to 8PM ✦ Closed SUNDAY

# A Day in the Life of a Pâtissier

AT 6AM, THE KITCHEN OF BOULANGERIE-PÂTISSERIE JULIEN IS IN FULL SWING, BUT THERE IS ALMOST NO CONVERSATION. *PÂTISSIERS* AND ASSISTANTS WORK SILENTLY, QUICKLY FILLING TART SHELLS WITH CREAM, PULLING TRAYS OF HARD-BAKED MERINGUES OUT OF THE OVEN, AND SPRINKLING POWDERED SUGAR ON BITE-SIZED, CREAM-DOLLOPED *NIFLETTES*.

Thirty-one-year-old head pastry chef Stephane Varin is just starting his day. He surveys the work of Christophe, who opened the kitchen at 2 a.m., and now masterfully garnishes strawberry tarts, spiraling the red berries from the center outwards. Varin eyes rows of *macarons* awaiting their ganache filling. He counts stacked trays of steaming, puffed *pains aux raisins* cooling before being sent upstairs to feed the morning's first hungry customers.

As the front of the shop prepares to open, cases are stocked with breads, *viennoiserie*, and a few fruit tarts. Madame Julien, in charge of the counter, calls down over the intercom for more *pains au chocolat* before they unlock the doors and the rush begins.

Back down in the kitchen, the *viennoiserie* chef cuts the raw croissant dough, places two chocolate *batonettes* on each rectangle, then rolls them up inside. On another counter, his assistant forms the same pastry dough into triangles, and rolls them into crescent form. All are loaded onto trays to await baking.

Varin jumps in to help glaze chocolate éclairs, twenty-five of them, and does a quick count of how many coffee and vanilla to prepare. He sorts through the day's orders, studying and prioritizing the morning's work. There are several early morning orders for trays of *viennoiserie* for nearby businesses, and twelve *entremets* (whole cakes or tarts for more than one person) that must be ready for the afternoon. (That's about average for a weekday—Saturdays average forty-six *entremets* to prepare!) Forty-eight brioches, eight *forêt noires*, twenty *flans natures*, ten each apricot and cherry, eight each coconut and chocolate. He starts with the flans, slicing large round cakes into triangular wedges, wiping his knife blade after every cut to keep the slices neat.

✦ At 7:40 a.m., Varin ducks out for a cigarette break and the second of five espressos he drinks each day. It's pitch dark and pouring rain as he slips into the fluorescent-lit café next door, and greets the bartender by name. He shakes hands with butchers in bloodied aprons, men in ties, and street cleaners in orange vests, throws back a quick *café*, inhales his cigarette, calls *"bonne journée"* to the crowd, and races back to his work.

On his way back downstairs to the *pâtisserie*, he passes through the *boulangerie*, where the shop's bread is prepared. Two flour-covered, white-faced *boulangers* are heaving dough out of oversized mixing bowls and shaping them into baguettes. By the end of the day, they will turn out more than 4,000 of Julien's award-winning loaves.

✦ At 9 a.m., the intercom loudspeaker roars from the shop, demanding more croissants, and a mini crisis ignites—there is no new batch in the oven. Varin quickly pulls a tray of raw dough triangles and pops it in, but it'll be at least twenty minutes before they're ready, he says. He reprimands the apprentice for sleeping on the job.

✦ At 9:45, the focus shifts from morning goods to afternoon favorites. Varin torches a large rectangular mold to remove the frozen *royal* cake within, then cuts it into individual servings. He gently removes gold leaf from thin paper sheets and sprinkles it onto chocolate-coated *Opéra* wedges. He tops the *poire chocolat mousse* pastries with chocolate shavings and a pear slice.

He removes a tray containing a giant *millefeuille* from the freezer where it's been cooling for a half hour, just long enough so it's cold (but not frozen) for slicing, a trick to keep cream and pastry layers intact. Varin expertly slices it into individual rectangular wedges, trims the edges, then dips the knife blade in the stove flame and brands each slice with a black diagonal mark across the white glazed top.

By 10 a.m., all the day's pastries are finished and upstairs in the cases. The kitchen is cleaned, the 2 a.m. shift removes their aprons, shakes colleagues' hands, and heads home. Varin and his remaining crew turn their attention to prep for the next day and rest of the week.

Today being Wednesday, the task at hand is *montage*, assembling the tart shells and molds with the biscuits, cakes, and crusts that have been prepared and frozen on Monday and Tuesday. Tomorrow, Thursday, they will prepare the mousses and fillings, and start work on the weekend's cake orders. Fridays are reserved for garnishes and decorative touches. Delicate pastry creams must be prepared daily—that's the early shift's first job when they arrive.

Before leaving, the apprentices must prepare for tomorrow's pastry case restocking. They set to work making two each of apricot, pear, apple "*grande-mere*," apple compote, and rhubarb tarts, and one each of plum, red berry, and apple rhubarb. They then freeze twenty-two trays of croissants for tomorrow's early morning shift to pull out and start baking.

Finally, at 1:15 p.m., "*On attaque le ménage*" ("We attack the clean up"), Varin says, as he and his crew spray down the entire space, wiping down every fridge, stove, and countertop. He does a quick check of raw materials, placing orders for stocks that are low, before heading home at 2 p.m.

# Boulangerie Pâtisserie Yannick Martin

302, RUE SAINT-HONORÉ, 1ST ARR.

Telephone ✦ 01 42 60 58 61

Métro ✦ TUILERIES

Open MONDAY through SATURDAY 7AM to 8PM

A RUE SAINT HONORÉ SHOPPING EXCURSION ISN'T COMPLETE WITHOUT STOPPING HERE FOR A *CROUSTI POIRE FRAMBOISE*, pear and raspberry jam sandwiched in between a slice of moist almond cake and a *sablé* biscuit. The *crousti* is unusual among delicate, refined French pastries for its gooey, sugary (and messy) appeal. The *Saint-Roch*, an almond shortbread cookie with orange cream, is another uncommonly sweet specialty. Chocolate fans should try the *César*, a chocolate mousse with chocolate cookie crust, and the *macaronade*, a chocolate *macaron* with buttery cream coffee pistachio filling.

# Charles Chocolatier

15, RUE MONTORGUEIL, 1ST ARR.

Telephone ✦ 01 45 08 57 77

Métro ✦ ETIENNE MARCEL

Open TUESDAY through SUNDAY 10AM to 7:45PM ✦ Closed MONDAY

LOCAL RESIDENTS SWEAR BY THE CHOCOLATES AT THIS SHOP AS THE BEST IN PARIS. FOR SERIOUS CHOCOLATE LOVERS ONLY; don't look for anything other than pure dark chocolate here, as Charles doesn't sell milk or white varieties. Specialty *bûches* are "logs" of dark chocolate with hazelnut and whole pistachios. Chocolate *macarons*, temptingly displayed in the front window, are the neighborhood favorite.

# Deliziefollie

7, RUE MONTORGUEIL, 1ST ARR.

*Telephone* ✦ 01 40 26 06 00

*Métro* ✦ LES HALLES

*Call for hours*

ELIZIEFOLLIE'S LUSCIOUS *GELATO* HAS WON OVER PARISIANS TO ITALIAN-STYLE ICE CREAM. EVER CONSCIENTIOUS about overindulging in rich treats but not willing to sacrifice taste, Parisians love *gelato*, perceived as Italy's lighter alternative to French *glace*, which is usually rich in cream and eggs. (See sidebar.) Deliziefollie's *gelato* is made fresh from a base of fresh milk and sugar. And that's all, according to shop staff. The specialty flavor is *Tentazione*, dark chocolate with chunks of ginger. My favorite is *Elizir*, a not-too-sour lime-and-basil sorbet that is the ultimate refreshment on a hot day.

Deliziefollie offers more than thirty flavors, including *gelato* classics and creative flavors, fresh fruit sorbets, and *granitas*. Deliziefollie is also one of the few, if only, Paris *glaciers* to offer "light" ice cream flavors, and they aren't bad.

# Ice Cream:
## French Glace Versus Italian Gelato

WITH ITALIAN-STYLE GELATERIAS SPRINGING UP AROUND PARIS, JOINING LOCAL ARTISANAL ICE CREAM MAKERS AND OFFERING UNLIMITED FLAVOR CHOICES, IT HELPS TO UNDERSTAND HOW ICE CREAM'S NATIONALITY AFFECTS IT TASTE AND CONSISTENCY.

Ice cream's origins are debated, but there is little doubt that Italians perfected it, and by the Renaissance it was widely consumed across Italy. Legends say that young Italian Catherine de Medici brought the popular treat to France when she arrived from Florence to marry future king Henry II in 1534. The French adapted the creamy delicacy to their tastes, distinguishing *glace* from *gelato*.

Although recipes vary widely, original Italian *gelato* is made from whole milk and doesn't contain any cream or eggs. Today, many recipes add cream and sometimes egg yolks, but purists insist on whole milk only. Generally, *gelato* has a butterfat content of 4-8%, depending on whether or not (and how much) cream is added. Varieties without cream contain about 4% butterfat. (By comparison, American ice creams contain anywhere from 8% for soft-serve to 18% butterfat for gourmet, luxury brands. French ice cream's content is in between the two.)

*Gelato*'s base ingredients and proportions depend on flavor. *Crema*, or Italian vanilla, is one variety that calls for fresh eggs, while yogurt flavor is made with fresh yogurt and no milk or cream at all. The creamy consistency comes from freezing techniques that maintain indirect cooling at a ready-to-serve soft temperature. For this reason, *gelato* is delicate and is best made fresh every day.

French recipes add cream and eggs, creating a denser, richer result. Its consistency is harder, softening around the outside as it melts. Because of the fresh eggs, it is also best consumed right away, with artisanal French producers making batches fresh every day.

# Les Gourmandises Parisiennes

TUILERIES GARDENS, next to the CENTRAL FOUNTAIN in the EAST END
(CLOSEST to the LOUVRE), 1ST ARR.
Open EVERY DAY APRIL through OCTOBER, 10:30AM to 7PM weather permitting

THIS UNASSUMING TUILERIES ICE CREAM STAND TURNS OUT TO BE THE OLDEST *GLACIER* IN PARIS, FOUNDED IN 1853 by Napoleon III's ice cream maker. Once having served France's Emperor, *Les Gourmandises Parisiennes* now delights park-goers with creamy gourmet flavors like praline, peach, pear, and Carambar. With a rotating selection of 200 *parfums*, specialties include *crème brulée* and violet. My favorite is the mint sorbet—a cone in front of the fountain is a refreshing treat on a summer day. Ice cream is made in the company's original factory in Seine-et-Marne outside of the city and is brought daily to its three park concession locations.

### ✦ ✦ ✦ Additional Locations ✦ ✦ ✦

LUXEMBOURG GARDENS, next to the *PÉTANQUE* COURTS
toward the SOUTHWESTERN CORNER, 6TH ARR.

SQUARE TINO ROSSI, 5TH ARR.
Métro FILLES DU CALVAIRE

# Hotel Ritz Paris

15, PLACE VENDÔME, 1ST ARR.

*Telephone* ✦ 01 43 16 33 63

*Métro* ✦ OPÉRA, TUILERIES

*Tea* EVERY DAY 4PM to 6PM

THE THIRD OF LOUIS XIV'S ROYAL SQUARES, PLACE VENDÔME HAS ALWAYS BEEN PARIS' CENTER OF CONSPICUOUS WEALTH. For a taste of this pampered world, treat yourself to afternoon tea at the Ritz, one of the square's most prominent residents.

The experience here is reserved and elegant, but pleasant. From the moment you step into the luxurious, cozy room, the friendly service puts you at ease and the hushed atmosphere turns from intimidating to relaxing. Several fixed tea menus offer selections of *petits fours* and tea sandwiches, or you can order à la carte. Inquire about the *pâtisserie* selections *du jour*, tarts and cakes made by the Ritz's top pastry chef.

You know you are in good hands when you order a favorite dessert you've had again and again, and are still thrilled by its perfection. A classic raspberry tart is piled high with berries over pastry cream, centered on a crunchy *sablé* crust. Other well-turned-out classics include a beautiful bowl of fresh fruit with cream, and the *religieuse*, a chocolate- and cream-filled pastry coated in chocolate icing. The *tarte exotique* is another delicious *sablé* crust smothered with a passion fruit mousse and bits of pineapple. If you are really hungry, the menu's *touches salées* (savory touches) include a club sandwich or *croque-monsieur* (at twenty-two euros, likely the most expensive grilled cheese in Paris).

In nice weather, enjoy the garden courtyard, one of Paris' prettiest. On a cold, gray day, have the famous *chocolat tradition Ritz* for "*les plus gourmands*," rich hot chocolate with caramel crunch ice cream. If you don't consider yourself one of the *plus gourmands*, try a simple gingerbread cake accompanied by a pot of orange zest hot chocolate. Reservation suggested.

# Jean-Paul Hevin

231, RUE SAINT-HONORÉ, 1ST ARR.

Telephone ✦ 01 55 35 35 96

Métro ✦ TUILERIES

Open MONDAY through SATURDAY 10AM to 7:30PM

Tea Salon NOON to 6:30PM ✦ Closed SUNDAY

I F EVER THERE WAS A CHIC *CHOCOLATIER*, JEAN-PAUL HEVIN IS IT. ON RUE SAINT-HONORÉ, THE HEART OF THE PARISIAN fashion world, this sleek boutique and *salon de thé* will satisfy any fashionista's urge for a chocolate fix. *Chez* Hevin, chocolate attains new levels of sophistication and passion. Always incredibly fresh and made from the highest quality beans, you can almost convince yourself it's good for you. (Some argue it is.)

If the beautifully formed shapes and grown-up flavors like rum-soaked raisin or dark chocolate espresso aren't enough to tempt you, the chocolate gift box will. With a choice of a love-, beauty- or chocolate-themed poem printed on the box, its stylish, pretty design is so appealing that you find yourself inventing a reason to put together a sampling for your *cheri(e)*. Eager to help, the friendly staff recommends dark solid blocks for purists (or those looking for health benefits) or lychee or honey-filled varieties for the adventurous.

Specialty pastries are, of course, all chocolate. The most intense is the *Guayaquil*, a chocolate crust topped with extra bitter chocolate mousse. The *Bergam* has a crunchy chocolate almond crust, with bergamot chocolate mousse, orange *crème brulée* custard, and flaky layers of crunchy praline inside. If you like praline, try the

*Longchamp praliné*, layered with hazelnut cake, praline cream, and meringue. Non-chocolate lovers, try the *gâteau fromage blanc*.

Offering a minimum of thirty different pastries from which to choose every day, as well as salads, omelets, and sandwiches for those who want savory before delving into the sweets, the *salon de thé* is a nice spot for sampling.

### ✦ ✦ ✦ Additional Locations ✦ ✦ ✦

3, RUE VAVIN, 6TH ARR.

Telephone 01 43 54 09 85 ✦ Métro VAVIN

Open TUESDAY through SATURDAY 10AM to 7PM

Closed SUNDAY and MONDAY


23 BIS, AVENUE DE LA MOTTE-PICQUET, 7TH ARR.

Telephone 01 45 51 77 48 ✦ Métro ECOLE MILITAIRE

Open TUESDAY to SATURDAY 10AM to 7:30PM

Closed SUNDAY and MONDAY

# Philippe Gosselin

125, RUE SAINT-HONORÉ, 1ST ARR.

Telephone ✦ 01 45 08 03 59

Métro ✦ LOUVRE-RIVOLI

Open SUNDAY through FRIDAY 7AM to 8PM ✦ Closed SATURDAY

GOSSELIN, AS THIS *BOULANGERIE* IS KNOWN, IS A SOLID ADDRESS TO KNOW ALONG THIS RUE ST.-HONORÉ STRETCH between Les Halles and the Louvre. Neighborhood locals swear by its *pâtisseries* and breads, claiming they are among the best in the area. Although I've never been wowed by the shop's sweets, it's safe to say all the classics here are reliably good — flans, *palmiers*, *sablés*, *religieuse*, *Paris-Brest*, *Opéra*. The éclair is a specialty, featured in a multicolored selection of flavors — rose, passion fruit, pistachio, even poppy flower, and of course vanilla, chocolate, and coffee. Gosselin's real pride and joy is its baguette. The shop has a huge selection of sandwiches, quiches, and pizzas to take away for lunch. And an entire side of the shop is dedicated to its house-made chocolates.

### ✦ ✦ ✦ Additional Location ✦ ✦ ✦

258, BOULEVARD SAINT-GERMAIN, 7TH ARR.

Telephone 01 45 51 53 11 ✦ Métro SOLFÉRINO

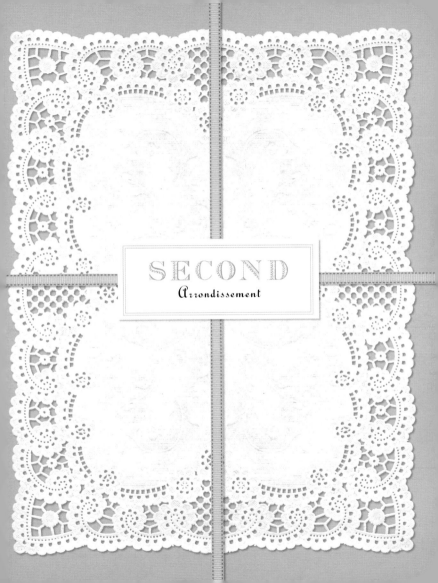

# SECOND
## Arrondissement

# A Priori Thé

35–37, GALERIE VIVIENNE, 2<sup>ND</sup> ARR.

Telephone ✦ 01 42 97 48 75

Métro ✦ BOURSE or PALAIS ROYAL-MUSÉE DU LOUVRE

Open MONDAY through FRIDAY 9AM to 6PM, SATURDAY 9AM to 6:30PM

SUNDAY NOON to 6:30PM

THIS TEAROOM'S ECLECTIC MENU REFLECTS THE INTERNATIONAL TASTES OF ITS TWO AMERICAN FOUNDERS. AMERICAN-style cheesecake and thick brownie squares are found among the raspberry almond tarts and *fromage blanc*. The menu changes frequently, and there are always interesting, original options. The teas are more predictable, with a selection of *grands classiques* like Darjeeling and Ceylon or green and herbal teas. Desserts are available in half-portions, nice for the undecided who want to taste a few.

The lunch menu also varies, with recent choices including a cantal tomato or leek cheddar *tourte*, an omelet soufflé with chevre and basil, lemon chicken with green beans and grilled zucchini, or *Welsh mountain* —another international nod—a ham, cheddar, and potato bake.

A Priori Thé is located in the delightfully restored Galerie Vivienne, one of Paris' most beautiful nineteenth-century *passages*, the "see and be seen" covered shopping arcade that was popular among turn-of-the-century *parisiennes*. Reserve a table for lunch and take in the décor and shops.

# Au Panetier

10, PLACE DES PETITS PÈRES, 2<sup>ND</sup> ARR.

Telephone ✦ 01 42 60 90 23

Métro ✦ SENTIER

Open MONDAY through FRIDAY 7:45AM to 7:15PM

Closed SATURDAY and SUNDAY

TUCKED BEHIND PLACE DES VICTOIRES, MY FAVORITE PARIS SQUARE, IS JEWEL-BOX *BOULANGERIE* AU PANETIER, MY preferred breakfast spot. The *pain au chocolat blanc* is the star attraction here. A unique creation, this doughy roll oozing with melted buttery white chocolate chunks is an intimidating caloric splurge, but one with a loyal following from all over Paris. The milk chocolate and caramel version of the roll is also special, although some find it too sweet.

Also original at Au Panetier are the *financiers*. Piled in glass jars on the countertop, they look suspiciously like muffins, but their luscious richness is distinctively the almond cake *financier*, the popular French mid-afternoon snack normally identifiable by its rectangular shape. Try the caramel, *groseilles* (currant), or chocolate ones. Au Panetier's uncommon brioche, speckled with raisins and dark chocolate bits, is satisfying and not too sugary.

For a true treat, have a *café crème* with

your *pain au chocolat blanc* and take in the mosaic tiled walls and molded ceiling dating from 1896. The beautiful Art Nouveau moment in Parisian *pâtisserie* and café décor inspired the brightly colored floral motifs and a scene including birds, fruit trees, and a château in the countryside, all splendidly preserved and on view as you sip your coffee in Au Panetier's tiny *salle à manger*.

At 2.60 euros for a *café crème* and *viennoiserie* of choice, less than the price of a simple coffee at most cafés, Au Panetier is one of Paris' best breakfast bargains. In season, a few sidewalk tables overlook pretty place des Petits Pères.

# G. Detou

58, RUE TIQUETONNE, 2ND ARR.

Telephone ✦ 01 42 36 54 67

Métro ✦ ETIENNE MARCEL or LES HALLES

Open MONDAY through SATURDAY 8:30AM to 6:30PM ✦ Closed SUNDAY

G. DETOU HAS BEEN SUPPLYING SERIOUS (AND NOT-SO-SERIOUS) *PÂTISSIERS* WITH EVERY IMAGINABLE INGREDIENT SINCE 1954. Shelves are stocked with tubs of liquid clarified butter, bags of nuts, candied ginger, saffron and hard-to-find spices, and dozens of types of sugar. You'll learn that the type of sugar used to caramelize a *tarte Tatin* is not the type used to top a *choquette*, nor is the chocolate used to make mousse the one used to make hot chocolate. The expert staff's advice is helpful and fun. G. Detou also offers cooking ingredients and French *produits de terroir*, traditional French regional food products that make great gifts.

G. Detou is near Les Halles, traditionally France's center of food culture, formerly the city's food market, now a neighborhood of wonderful restaurant/kitchen supply stores. This is the quarter to find *madeleine* pans, *tarte Tatin* pans, heavy copper pots, *sauciers*, café-style water carafes, cheese serving plates, onion soup bowls, and whatever else you need.

# Stohrer

51, RUE MONTORGEUIL, 2ND ARR.

*Telephone* ✦ 01 42 33 38 20

*Métro* ✦ ETIENNE MARCEL or LES HALLES

*Open* DAILY 7:30AM to 8:30PM

EVEN IF YOU CAN'T MAKE THE DAY TRIP TO VERSAILLES, YOU CAN TAKE A SMALL STEP INTO EIGHTEENTH-CENTURY French royal life by sampling Stohrer's *puits d'amour* and famous *baba au rhum.* These two revered house recipes were likely favorites of Louis XV when Nicolas Stohrer was the royal *pâtissier.* When Stohrer left the court in 1730, he took his recipes with him and established this *pâtisserie*, today one of Paris' oldest, on a now-trendy market street. These pastries, unlike many eighteenth-century tastes, have withstood the test of time and Stohrer still sells them, true to their original, closely guarded formula.

*Puits d'amours*, or "wells of love"

(sadly, owner Francois Duthu doesn't know the origins of the name), are small, round puff pastries filled with vanilla cream and caramel. Stohrer's other original creation, the *baba au rhum*, caught on among Parisians and is now a classic. Stohrer sells three types: the original *baba au rhum* (a brioche filled with pastry cream and rum), the *ali baba* (with raisins), and the *baba chantilly* (topped with a dollop of whipped cream).

Other local favorites are the *tarte à l'orange*, a crumbly shortbread tart with tangy orange cream filling, *tarte aux fraises des bois* (wild strawberry tart), and the *millefeuille*. Serious chocolate lovers shouldn't miss the *criolo*, a 55%-pure chocolate dessert of chocolate mousse, layers of chocolate biscuit, and almond cake.

The shop itself is worth a visit, featuring a beautiful painted glass ceiling added in 1864 by master artisan Paul Baudry, who also worked on the front hall of Paris' splendid Opéra Garnier. If you are a fan of this style décor, don't miss an opera house tour (every day 10 a.m. to 5 p.m. except Sunday). Even better, snag a last-minute, cheap seat to that evening's performance. Tickets are available directly at the box office.

# Les Crèmes:
## Deciphering what's inside all those pastries

ONE OF THE FIRST LESSONS FOR ANY ASPIRING *PÂTISSIER* IS *LES CRÈMES*, THE BASE OF ALMOST ALL FRENCH PASTRIES. UNDERSTANDING THE DIFFERENT CREAMS CAN ALSO BE HANDY KNOWLEDGE FOR AMATEUR PASTRY EATERS, HELPING TO CRACK THE CODE ON WHAT'S INSIDE ALL THOSE LUSCIOUS LOOKING PUFFS IN THE PASTRY CASE.

◆ *CRÈME CHANTILLY* is simple whipped cream, heavy cream beaten with sugar and sometimes a little vanilla extract (sometimes also called *crème fouettée*).

◆ *CRÈME PÂTISSIÈRE* is the fundamental cream base for almost all recipes, at the center of éclairs, *millefeuille*, Paris-Brest, and many fruit tarts. It is made with milk, egg, sugar, butter, and "*crème pâtissière* powder," which is a cornstarch-like thickener. *Crème pâtissière* can be mixed with chocolate or coffee to make a chocolate or coffee cream (as for éclairs.)

◆ *CRÈME D'AMANDE*, a rich almond cream made with egg and equal parts butter, sugar, and almond powder, is often featured in fruit tarts like strawberry and some apple varieties, and many chocolate- or nut-based recipes.

◆ *CRÈME AU BEURRE* is made by beating butter into *crème pâtissière*. To offset its richness, it is frequently used in combination with other creams. For example, the classic strawberry dessert, the *fraisier*, contains both *crème au beurre* and *crème pâtissière* layered on a sponge cake (*biscuit genoise*) with fresh berries.

- *CRÈME MOUSSELINE* is a mix of one-third *crème au beurre* and two-thirds part *crème pâtissière*.

- *FRANGIPANE*, the classic cream filling for the New Year's *galette des rois*, is one-third *crème pâtissière* and two-thirds part *crème d'amande*.

- *CRÈME ANGLAISE*, a heavy, egg yolk-based liquid cream, is often used as a garnish for desserts like crêpes or chocolate cakes.

- *CRÈME GLACÉE* is ice cream.

# THIRD

## Arrondissement

# La Fougasse

25, RUE DE BRETAGNE, 3RD ARRONDISSEMENT

Telephone ✦ 01 42 72 36 80

Métro ✦ FILLES DU CALVAIRE

Open TUESDAY through SATURDAY 7AM to 8PM

SUNDAY 7AM to 2PM ✦ Closed MONDAY

STOP IN FOR A LA FOUGASSE *SABLÉ* IF YOU FIND YOURSELF NEAR RUE DE BRETAGNE, THE 3RD ARRONDISSEMENT'S well-known market street, with an array of *fromageries, traiteurs*, fruit vendors, and the Marché des Enfants Rouges, Paris' oldest covered market. The *sablés* come out of the kitchen on wide sheets and are cut into crumbly, buttery squares. Choose between raspberry jam or lemon curd fillings. Other good options are the specialty *Magellan*, a lime-infused chocolate and hazelnut layered cake on *biscuit génoise*, or the deliciously rich *royal*, chocolate mousse and praline *feuilleté* layers topping an almond biscuit crust.

The *Saint Tropeziane*, a brioche sandwiching *mousseline* cream, is a neighborhood Sunday breakfast favorite. La Fougasse also makes a good croissant.

# Au Levain de Marais

32, RUE DE TURENNE, 3<sup>RD</sup> ARR.

_Telephone_ ✦ 01 42 78 07 31

_Métro_ ✦ CHEMIN VERT

_Open_ TUESDAY _through_ SATURDAY 7AM _to_ 8:30PM

_Closed_ SUNDAY _and_ MONDAY

PLACE DES VOSGES IS PERHAPS PARIS' BEST PICNIC SPOT, AND HAPPILY, AU LEVAIN DE MARAIS, ONE OF THE RESIDENTS' favorite *boulangeries*, has shops on either side of the square. It's hard to go wrong here with sweets or savories, but my highest recommendations go to the lemon and lime tarts. The filling is creamy and smooth, sweet and tart at the same time. The shop's croissants are extra flaky and super buttery, with a loyal following who claim them as their favorite. The *tulipe au chocolat*, an original creation of chocolate mousse in a chocolate-covered *tuile* cookie shell, doesn't look as pretty as other options, but is surprisingly good. The brioche and the fig cake are also excellent.

For picnic savories, the wrap with spinach and goat cheese (called a *flammenkuche*) is a bit messy but delicious. Be sure to ask to have it

heated. The baguette (Au Levain de Marais' specialty) is good enough to devour on its own, particularly when it's still warm.

Opening hours alternate between the two shops, so you need never go without one of Au Levain de Marais' lemon tarts when the craving hits.

### ✦ ✦ ✦ Additional Locations ✦ ✦ ✦

28, BOULEVARD BEAUMARCHAIS, 11TH ARR.
Telephone 01 48 05 17 14 ✦ Métro CHEMIN VERT or BASTILLE
Open THURSDAY through MONDAY 7AM to 8:30PM
Closed TUESDAY and WEDNESDAY

✳

142, AVENUE PARMENTIER, 11TH ARR.
Telephone 01 43 57 36 91 ✦ Métro GONCOURT
Open TUESDAY through SATURDAY 7AM to 8:30PM
Closed SUNDAY and MONDAY

✳

48, RUE CAULAINCOURT, 18TH ARR.
Telephone 01 46 06 96 71 ✦ Métro LAMARCK-CAULAINCOURT
Call for hours

# Perfect Picnic Spots

### Place Dauphine, 1ST ARR.

THIS SQUARE IS A TINY OASIS, tucked on the tip of busy Ile de la Cité, just off Pont Neuf and behind the Palais de Justice. According to legend, actor Yves Montagne played *pétanque*, the French bowling game, here daily in his old age.

### La Cour Carrée at the Louvre, 1ST ARR.

THIS ENCLOSED COURTYARD at the eastern end of the Louvre is my favorite spot for a *petit repos*. At any time of day, large, flat benches are bathed in sun, and in the evening the museum's lighting stunningly showcases the building's architecture. The sounds of music performers under the arches and the fountain at the square's center are the perfect antidote for a busy day.

### Pont des Arts, 1ST and 6TH ARRS.

EXIT THE COUR CARRÉE'S SOUTH (RIVER) SIDE, and you'll find yourself facing the Pont des Arts, a pedestrian bridge that turns into a sunset watchers' *rendez-vous* on summer evenings. Views in all directions show off Paris' sightseeing highlights. Here, you are perfectly poised to enjoy views of most every major Paris monument. Don't forget the champagne!

### Jardin du Palais Royal, 1ST ARR.

CENTRAL PARIS' HIDDEN GEM, even those who know its location can struggle to find an entrance through the arcades. (The easiest way is through place Colette, by the Palais-Royal Musée du Louvre métro station.) The peaceful gardens, fountains, and historic buildings surrounding the square are breathtaking. If you don't have picnic supplies, try one of the outdoor cafés.

### The Quais on Sunday, 1ST and 4TH ARRS.

ON SUNDAYS, Paris' river quais are closed to traffic and open to strollers, bikers, roller bladers—and picnickers. One favorite stretch-out site is the grassy, tree-lined spot on the Right Bank facing Ile Saint-Louis.

### Square Jean XXIII behind Notre Dame, 1ST ARR.

THIS LOVELY GARDEN behind the famous cathedral is much quieter than the touristy square in front, with arguably just as good a view. Shaded benches and impressive roses and flowerbeds make it a nice point to pause before or after battling the church-visiting crowds. It's also convenient to Ile Saint-Louis.

### The Banks of Ile Saint-Louis, 4TH ARR.

THE BANKS OF ILE SAINT-LOUIS rank as one of Paris' most romantic spots to set up for an evening *apéritif*. Join locals sipping champagne and watching the *bateaux mouches* pass as the sun goes down. The most coveted spot is at the westernmost tip of the island (with views of Hôtel de Ville and Ile de la Cité). To get down to the riverbank, take any of the stairways from the street.

### Square Tino Rossi, 5TH ARR.

(ENTER *from* QUAI SAINT BERNARD. A PEDESTRIAN PATH RUNS DOWN *to the* RIVER *just after* PONT DE SULLY.)

ONE OF PARIS' PRETTIEST SEINE VIEWS, facing Ile Saint-Louis and the back spires of Notre Dame, this park has a lively evening outdoor music and dance scene. Watch a tango lesson, or better yet join in!

### Jardin des Plantes, 5TH ARR.

ONE OF PARIS' MOST UNDERRATED and little-known parks, this botanical garden is a nice place for a stroll and a bite. It has a charming carousel with animals fashioned on the rare species in the National History Museum behind it, and an animal menagerie for kids.

### Rue de Seine, Square G. Pierne, 6TH ARR.

THIS IS A CONVENIENT LITTLE STOPPING POINT to quickly eat purchases from rue de Seine's nearby *boulangeries* and to-go sandwich shops. Don't miss the whimsical design of the benches in the form of open books.

# Maison Brocco

180, RUE DU TEMPLE, 3RD ARR.

Telephone ✦ 01 42 72 19 81

Métro ✦ RÉPUBLIQUE

Open MONDAY through SATURDAY 6:30AM to 8PM ✦ Closed SUNDAY

I HAD WALKED PAST THIS NEIGHBORHOOD *BOULANGERIE-PÂTISSERIE* MANY TIMES, DISMISSING IT AS NOTHING SPECIAL. Then one afternoon, craving a sweet as I dashed to the République métro, I discovered Maison Brocco's *choquettes*. These mini pastry puffs, light but not airy, with a chewy, popover-like texture, are perfectly bite-sized.

I should know by now that you can't judge a *pâtisserie* by its façade—Maison Brocco turns out to be one of the best spots in my neighborhood. Its generic look and unglamorous location on a busy strip of discount stores doesn't betray the exceptional goodies inside.

Maison Brocco's specialty is *le royale*, a dense chocolate and pastry cream concoction with a crunchy, biscuit crust. The non-chocolate version, a hazelnut biscuit topped with pastry cream, is just as good. Both are worthy of the title house specialty. I'm hooked on the buttery, vanilla-tinged *madeleines*. Sold in bags of ten, I'm told they keep for up to a week, but my bag never lasts more than two days. All of the *viennoiserie* at the popular outside counter here are excellent—the croissants, *pains au chocolate*, *pain aux raisins*. Brioches are thick and golden, with serious "teeth-sinking" appeal. The thick irresistible slices of *gâteau au fromage blanc*, the cheesecake made with whipped, creamy yogurt-style cheese, are dense yet light and completely satisfying.

# The Madeleine: A Snack Time Classic

AFTERNOONS, AROUND 4:30, THE LINES START FORMING OUTSIDE *PÂTISSERIES*. IT'S *GOÛTER*—SNACK TIME—WHEN CHILDREN ACCOMPANIED BY PARENTS AND NANNIES FILE INTO SHOPS FOR THEIR DAILY SWEET TREAT. *PAINS AU CHOCOLAT*, *QUATRE QUARTS*, CAKES, AND *SABLÉS* ARE FAVORITES, BUT THE CLASSIC SNACK IS THE *MADELEINE*.

Easy to eat, kids enjoy them with milk, while adults dip them in tea. Some like them dry and crumbly. I prefer mine buttery and moist.

Made from eggs, sugar, flour, milk, and melted butter, this petit, shell-shaped teacake originated in the eighteenth century in the Lorraine. Some say the shell shape stems from its popularity along the pilgrimage route that passed through Commercy, the town of its origin. (The shell was the symbol of the pilgrimage.) Today, the *madeleine*'s history is most commonly linked with Marcel Proust who celebrated them in *Remembrance of Things Past*.

A plain *madeleine* is called a *madeleine nature*, but flavors can be added by including vanilla, lemon or orange zest, honey, rosewater, or chocolate powder.

*Pâtissiers* say they can gauge their client base on *madeleine* sales. They sell like hot cakes in residential areas with families and older populations of *grandes dames parisiennes* who enjoy their afternoon tea. By contrast, they languish on the counter of shops with a strong business and lunchtime clientele, taking a backseat to croissants and éclairs.

# Pain de Sucre

14, RUE RAMBUTEAU, 3$^{RD}$ ARR.

Telephone ✦ 01 45 74 68 92

Métro ✦ RAMBUTEAU

Open THURSDAY through MONDAY 8AM to 8:30PM

Closed TUESDAY and WEDNESDAY

SEVERAL YEARS AGO, MUCH TO MY SURPRISE, MARSHMALLOWS BEGAN TURNING UP ON THE MENUS OF HIP PARISIAN CHEFS. The soft, supple, homemade French *guimauves* (a good French word to know) hardly resemble the crusty, stale supermarket variety of my American childhood; the *fleur d'orange* homemade marshmallows from Pain de Sucre, a *pâtisserie* specializing in off-beat sweets, are melt-in-your-mouth clouds of delicate orange essence, delectable enough to tempt a skeptic like me. The chestnut honey version is gooey and soaked. Fluffy chocolate ones are yummy, but leave me craving more chocolate. I find the pistachio and angelica version has an unusual taste, perhaps because angelica (a plant used for flavoring sweets) is not something I eat often (or ever). The saffron and green tea varieties are interesting, but I'm not wild about them.

Pain de Sucre's unusual concepts are hard to resist, tempting you to taste bizarre combinations like endive and orange marmalade, brioche, beer mousse, and crumbled candied chestnuts (unappealingly called the *amertume* or "bitterness"). A more conservative choice might be the *tatigala*, almond pastry crust with praline cream, quince pulp, caramelized apple, and rosemary. Or try the *momo*, a hazelnut meringue, chocolate mousse with mango and passion fruit cream. If you're craving something tamer, go for the *pain d'épice*, the house specialty called the *Zanzibar*—a must. To translate *pain d'épice* as gingerbread doesn't do it justice. A dense, not-too-sweet cake made with honey and spices, depending on the recipe, *pain d'épice* can include anything from cinnamon, anise seed, or nutmeg, to orange zest. Pain de Sucre's recipe is heavy on the honey, chunky with pistachios, with a moist, dense texture resembling pumpkin or zucchini bread.

For the truly unadventurous, raspberry tarts and *millefeuille* are available. Chocolate lovers shouldn't miss the *état de choc* (state of shock), a dark chocolate cookie topped by chocolate ganache, again topped by chocolate cream. The *fleur d'orange* "mini-flan" is a thin *sablé* pastry crust coated with a layer of sweet orange flan.

# FOURTH

*Arrondissement*

# Amorino

47, RUE SAINT-LOUIS-EN-L'ILE, 4TH ARR.

Telephone ✦ 01 44 07 48 08

Métro ✦ PONT MARIE

Open EVERY DAY NOON to MIDNIGHT

SINCE THIS GELATERIA OPENED IN 2002, PARISIANS HAVE FLOCKED TO DEVOUR ITS ITALIAN-STYLE ICE CREAM. THE first shop on Ile St-Louis initially drew crowds as it was the only ice cream seller on the island with late-night hours and no line. The crowds became converts, and now the line snakes around the block. Amorino since has opened locations all over Paris to meet demand for this favorite Italian export.

Despite its expansion, Amorino's *gelato* remains exclusively homemade, necessary for its luscious, delicate texture and flavors. Amorino's not-to-miss specialties are *stracciatella* (chocolate chip), coffee, *amaretto* (almond biscuit), and *bacio* (chocolate and hazelnut), but its flavor roster includes all the Italian favorites like *crema* (a rich, Italian-style vanilla), chocolate, *nocciola* (hazelnut), *tiramisu*, *amarena* (vanilla with wild cherries), and yogurt. Sorbet staples include passion fruit, raspberry, pineapple, and more exotic flavors like "ACE" (orange, carrot, and lemon) and grapefruit rose.

Amorino on rue Vavin in the sixth arrondissement is just outside the gates of Luxembourg Gardens, a perfect spot to stroll with a cone. But be sure to get in line before 4:30 p.m., the school day's end and the traditional hour for *goûter*, French children's after-school snack.

# ✦ ✦ ✦ Additional Locations ✦ ✦ ✦

31, RUE VIEILLE DU TEMPLE, 4TH ARR.

Telephone 01 42 78 07 75 ✦ Métro HÔTEL DE VILLE

Open EVERY DAY NOON to MIDNIGHT

✦

82, RUE MONTORGUEIL, 2ND ARR.

Telephone 01 45 08 92 58 ✦ Métro ETIENNE MARCEL

Open EVERY DAY NOON to MIDNIGHT

✦

4, RUE DE BUCI, 6TH ARR.

Telephone 01 43 26 57 46 ✦ Métro ODEON

Open EVERY DAY NOON to MIDNIGHT

✦

4, RUE VAVIN, 6TH ARR.

Telephone 01 42 22 66 86 ✦ Métro VAVIN or NOTRE-DAME-DES-CHAMPS

Open EVERY DAY NOON to MIDNIGHT

✦

17, RUE DAGUERRE, 14TH ARR.

Telephone 01 43 20 15 78 ✦ Métro DENFERT-ROCHEREAU

Open DAILY NOON to MIDNIGHT

✦

35, BOULEVARD HAUSSMANN, 9TH ARR.

(on the GROUND FLOOR of LAFAYETTE MAISON)

Telephone 01 49 24 94 30 ✦ Métro HAVRE-CAUMARTIN

Open MONDAY through SATURDAY 9AM to 7:30PM

(9 P.M. on THURSDAY) ✦ Closed SUNDAY

# Berthillon

29–31, RUE SAINT-LOUIS-EN-L'ILE, 4TH ARR.

Telephone ◆ 01 43 54 31 61

Métro ◆ PONT MARIE

Open WEDNESDAY through SUNDAY 10AM to 8PM

Closed MONDAY and TUESDAY

BY FAR THE MOST FAMOUS NAME IN FRENCH ICE CREAM, BERTHILLON HAS ELEVATED THE CHILDHOOD TREAT TO *gastronomique* status in France. Some say the *glace* is over-rated, but its freshness and gourmet flavor selection were novel when it opened its doors in 1954. Nevertheless, the intensely-flavored ice cream's and fruit sorbet's fame was established, along with lifetime devotees and a reputation that continues to this day as Parisians and tourists line the sidewalks of Ile Saint-Louis to get a scoop or take away tub.

Berthillon's recipe's secret is in its purity—milk, *crème fraiche*, eggs, and sugar only—and in the quality of those ingredients. Flavors are created with all-natural ingredients, never from any additives. Special-ties include *chocolat noir*, *chocolat blanc* (both from the highest-quality chocolate), and *vanille*, made with vanilla beans from Madagascar. The sorbet's intense fruit flavors vary according to season. Try pear, wild strawberry, melon, or apricot. Today, Berthillon's ice cream is sold in its original Ile Saint-Louis *salon de thé* location and in cafés around Paris, but don't expect to cool down with a *boule* in July or August or on French school holidays, when the shop is shuttered in keeping with its traditional vacation schedule.

# Boulangerie Malineau

18, RUE VIEILLE DU TEMPLE, 4TH ARR.

*Telephone* ✦ 01 42 76 94 54

*Métro* ✦ HÔTEL DE VILLE OR SAINT-PAUL

*Open* MONDAY *through* FRIDAY 7:30AM *to* 9PM

SATURDAY *and* SUNDAY 8AM *to* 10PM ✦ *Closed* TUESDAY

BOULANGERIE MALINEAU'S UNIQUE SPECIALTY, *PAIN AU CHOCOLAT FRAMBOISE*, IS ALMOST ALWAYS SOLD OUT BY lunchtime. No matter, since they are best eaten fresh anyway while the chocolate and raspberry filling is still warm and oozing. If you prefer banana to raspberry, Malineau also has a *pain au chocolat banane*.

Forget fancy, picture-perfect pastries; Malineau only offers an extensive line-up of hearty *viennoiserie*, tarts, cakes, and *sablés*. The shop window shows off its unusual *sablés* of all shapes, colors, and sizes, such as the impressive checkerboard-patterned *sablé au chocolat pistache* or the pink and green checkered *pistache frambroise*. Likewise, choose from almost any seasonal fruit tart imaginable: peach, apricot, apple, pear, lemon (with or without meringue), quince, and berry, among others.

As a *boulangerie* specializing in breads,

Malineau is known for its *baguette parisienne*, and makes delicious whole grain, nut, and cheese breads. The rue Vieille du Temple location seems to specialize in Malineau's sweet selections, while the rue St.-Paul location a few blocks away has an impressive spread of quiches and savory tarts.

### ✦ ✦ ✦ Additional Locations ✦ ✦ ✦

26, RUE ST.-PAUL, 4TH ARR.

Telephone 01 48 87 64 10 ✦ Métro SAINT-PAUL

Open THURSDAY through TUESDAY 7AM to 8PM ✦ Closed WEDNESDAY

3, RUE VINEUSE, 16TH ARR.

Telephone 01 45 20 56 65 ✦ Métro PASSY

Open TUESDAY through SATURDAY 7AM to 8PM, SUNDAY 8AM to 8PM

Closed MONDAY

# Boulangerie Philippe Martin

40, RUE ST.-LOUIS-EN-L'ILE, 4TH ARR.

Telephone ✦ 01 43 54 69 48

Métro ✦ PONT MARIE

Open TUESDAY through SATURDAY 7:15AM to 1:30PM and 3:30PM to 8PM

Closed SUNDAY and MONDAY

PHILIPPE MARTIN MAKES ONE OF THE BEST CROISSANTS (FLAKY AND SWEET WITH A LIGHT TOUCH OF SALT) AND certainly the best baguette (especially baguette *à l'ancienne*) on the Ile Saint-Louis. The outstanding *viennoiserie* and breads highlight Martin's talent as a *boulanger*, but his pastries are strong too. The delicate *tarte aux figues* has four perfectly ripe fruit slices floating on pastry cream in a crunchy *sablé* shell. Lemon tarts are petite, but tasty and always fresh.

# Café Français

3, PLACE DE LA BASTILLE, 4TH ARR.

Telephone ✦ 01 40 29 04 02

Metro ✦ BASTILLE

Open DAILY 7AM to MIDNIGHT

CAFÉ FRANÇAIS LOOKS LIKE ANY OTHER OF THE *GRANDS CAFÉS* THAT LINE PARIS' PLACES AND BOULEVARDS, THIS one facing the Bastille monument. For pastry connoisseurs, however, it's a serious find—a café attached to an excellent *pâtisserie*. At last—a café where you can order a first-rate dessert with your coffee, a place where sweets are the focus. Three professional *pâtissiers* turn out fresh trays of croissants, tarts, and cakes from early morning to midnight. Famous for its *palmiers*, the kitchen adds an extra amount of rich salted butter to make the "elephant ears" exceptionally crisp and crunchy. The chefs' other specialty is the *millefeuille*. A light touch produces a smooth and whipped cream that is neatly slathered on sweet flaky pastry layers. My vote is for the *clafoutis*, a satisfying, pudding-like cake that combines eggs, sugar, and fruit combinations such as apple and caramel or pear and chocolate on a thick crust. Café Français also makes an excellent *royal*, chocolate mousse and *praline feuilleté* layered on an almond biscuit.

A simple café menu offers sandwiches, basic salads, *croque-monsieur*, a hamburger, and quiches. Desserts are the highlight here, *bien sûr*. In nice weather, the terrace spills over onto place de la Bastille, practically doubling seating capacity and creating a lively atmosphere for people watching.

# L'Ebouillante

6 RUE DES BARRES, 4TH ARR.

Telephone ✦ 01 42 71 09 69

Métro ✦ HÔTEL DE VILLE

Open TUESDAY through SUNDAY NOON to 10PM

(9PM in winter) ✦ Closed MONDAY

SAVORING A WARM SLICE OF *TARTE TATIN* BATHED IN THICK *CRÈME FRAICHE* ON L'EBOUILLANTE'S QUIET TERRACE IS about as good as it gets. Tucked on a cobbled pedestrian street behind the church of St. Gervais, this café/*crêperie* is a gem for a snack or light meal.

Sweet snacks are best, of course, with delicious tarts and cakes at the top of my recommendations. In addition to the *tarte Tatin*, the *tarte au citron* is a good choice, featuring a thick, satisfying layer of lemon curd. The chocolate and cinnamon hazelnut cakes are also favorites.

*Les cocktails glacés* (frozen non-alcoholic drinks) are refreshing on a warm day. With or without whipped cream, the *chocolat glacé* is rich with cocoa, milk, egg, and cream. The yogurt and apricot is smooth and sweet; cold milk with caramel is sugary and thick. *Pomme d'épices* is a light apple, orange, and lemon juice with cinnamon. When the air is nippy, go for a *café* sprinkled with cinnamon, ginger, or vanilla or a glass of warm milk with honey.

At lunchtime, Ebouillante's extensive savory menu lists excellent soups, salads, eggs, quiches, and crêpes. Giant sized crêpes, called "bricks" and made from Tunisian semolina flour, are stuffed with fillings like ham, tomato, cheese, mushrooms, and curry or *crème fraiche*, lemon, and smoked salmon. I love the *fromage blanc* with spinach, raisins, and nuts.

L'Ebouillante is best in nice weather when the terrace is open. Inside, the restaurant is cramped and lacks character.

# Tarte Tatin

THE LEGEND OF THE TATIN SISTERS AND THEIR ACCIDENTAL CREATION OF *TARTE TATIN*, THE NOW FAMOUS FRENCH "UPSIDE DOWN" APPLE TART, IS WELL ESTABLISHED. THE SISTERS' HOMETOWN OF LAMOTTE-BEUVRON CELEBRATES ITS MOST PROMINENT PROGENY AND RESIDENTS HAVE FORMED A SOCIETY TO PRESERVE THE TART'S HERITAGE.

The story tells of Stephanie and Caroline Tatin who ran the Hotel Tatin in this Loire Valley town. Stephanie, in charge of the kitchen, one day tried to salvage a tart by draping the crust over the top of caramelized apples after forgetting to place it on the bottom of the mold. It was a hit among customers and *voilà*— the *tarte Tatin* was born. (Taking the story one step further, some say the creation owes its fame to Maxim's restaurant's owner, who added the dessert to his Paris menu after tasting the sisters' version, thus solidifying its place in French gastronomic history.)

A classic *tarte Tatin* consists of gently caramelized apples, sautéed in butter and sugar on a stovetop, then topped with crust, baked, and carefully inverted after coming out of the oven. Apples should be thickly sliced (some say halved) and be firm, retaining their shape even after baking. Favorite French apple varieties are *Reine des Reinettes* or *Boskoop*. (The closest firm American apple is Golden Delicious.) Some chefs insist the secret is pressing the crust securely around the pan's side, sealing in the apples for baking.

*Tarte Tatin*'s thickness requires a special pan, deeper than a regular tart pan, and preferably thicker to prevent burning during carmelization. Traditionalists like skillets, but nonstick or flexible silicone pans can make the final flipping easier.

The classic recipe calls for *pâte brisée sucrée*, although some prefer a *pâte feuilletée* for variations with summer fruits, such as plums or peaches, which have lots of water. Non-dessert versions can use a simple *pâte brisée*.

Since the sister's original version in 1898, *tarte Tatin* has taken many forms, and today any tart, *sucrée* or *salée*, that is baked with the crust on top and then inverted, is labeled "Tatin." Purists may balk, but it's fun experimenting with pineapple, cherries, figs, currant berries, mango, even chocolate. For a main course, try spinach and feta, tomato and mozzarella, zucchini and herbs, or endive.

# Heurtier

2, RUE DE LA VERRERIE, 4TH ARR.

Telephone ◆ 01 40 27 91 97

Métro ◆ HÔTEL DE VILLE

Open TUESDAY through SUNDAY 9AM to 11PM ◆ Closed MONDAY

HEURTIER BILLS ITSELF AS A *BISTRO À PAINS*, A BOULAN-GERIE / RESTAURANT WITH A MENU BUILT AROUND ITS delicious breads and baked products. Heurtier's *viennoiserie* and perfect lunch, brunch, or tea menu of soups and gourmet sandwiches all feature the *boulangerie*'s tasty, interesting breads.

Heurtier's desserts are all excellent, the classics and more inventive choices alike. The pistachio and raspberry *financiers* are dense and buttery. The seasonal fig tart is perfectly crusty and sweet. I also give a strong review to the *gâteau au fromage*, dense and moist but still light. The hot chocolate or *chocolat maison* is so rich it's like drinking three liquid chocolate bars and bears no resemblance to the Hershey's Syrup variety.

The stylish, welcoming upstairs tearoom/restaurant is nice for lunch, with good service, nice music, and a view over the lively place des Baudoyer. The quiche lorraine is exceptional, as are the omelets and the *croque-monsieur*, all served with a green salad. A dreamy breakfast/brunch menu of specialty breads and *viennoiserie* is served until noon. The downstairs *boulangerie/pâtisserie* tends to have a better selection of desserts, so if you spot something that doesn't appear on the dessert menu, be sure to ask about it.

In season, Heurtier sells its creative ice cream flavors at a window in front of the shop.

# Le Loir dans la Théière

3, RUE DES ROSIERS, 4<sup>TH</sup> ARR.

*Telephone* ✦ 01 42 72 90 61

*Métro* ✦ SAINT-PAUL

*Open* MONDAY *through* FRIDAY 11:30AM *to* 7PM

SATURDAY *and* SUNDAY 10AM *to* 7PM

LE LOIR DANS LA THÉIÈRE IS ONE OF MY FAVORITE WEEKDAY LUNCH SPOTS. I SPECIFY WEEKDAY BECAUSE IT'S IMPOSsible to get a table during its wildly popular weekend brunch without enduring an endless wait. This is the type of place where everyone lingers and orders dessert.

For me, lunch starts with an in-depth examination of the dessert buffet. I work backwards, making my sweet selections first. The drawback to this strategy is that I spend the entire meal deliberating whether to order the mango cake or the *fondant chocolat à l'orange* (melted chocolate cake with orange).

I choose both and the mango cake is the more satisfying of the two, a buttery yellow cake with chunks of at least one large, perfectly ripe mango. On a return trip, I devour the chocolate banana tart. Other tasty options are the lemon tart (dripping with whipped spongy meringue), the *gâteau au fromage blanc* with pear and raisins, and a

favorite dense chocolate cake. The hot chocolate is perfectly "*maison*" (i.e., the real deal, no powder) without being too rich.

For lunch, I love a bowl of the always-delicious soup of the day, with *pain*, of course. If I'm starving I can usually polish off a piece of quiche and still have space for dessert. The fluffy quiches and *tourtes* are well-made, filled with creative ingredients, and served with a heaping salad. The lunch menu also features omelets and a pasta of the

day. There are always plenty of interesting veggie options, making this a good choice for vegetarians.

Le Loir dans la Théière is a great place to hole up on a gray day. Heavy draperies protect front tables from the doorway's draft, ensconcing you in what feels like grandmother's (albeit smoky) attic—perfect if it's rainy and cold outside. On my first visit I was nearly smoked out, but I loved the food so much that I returned, and happily discovered the non-smoking backroom.

# Mariage Frères

30 and 35, RUE BOURG-TIBOURG, 4TH ARR.

Telephone + 01 42 72 28 11

Métro + HÔTEL DE VILLE

Boutique EVERY DAY 10:30AM through 7:30PM

Tea Salon EVERY DAY NOON to 7PM

IF YOU WANT TO INDULGE, MARIAGE FRÈRES, ONE OF PARIS' OLDEST TEA SALONS, WITH A SELECTION OF MORE THAN 560 teas from all over the world and excellent pastries, is a good place to do so.

After hearing raves ("best dessert of my life"), I joined the pilgrimage to Mariage Frères, deciding to splurge on an afternoon sweet. Sipping tea and savoring my pastry, presented luxuriously on French porcelain china with silver service, was pleasant, but most of the cakes were simply too fussy for my taste. I kept returning to Mariage Frères, trying to share others' enthusiasm, but I could never quite find the perfect pastry to fulfill the satisfying, sugar-indulging experience I crave.

Then one rainy afternoon, following the lead of well-coifed *parisiennes* at the neighboring table, I asked about *le chariot*. A fancy cart was wheeled over to my table, and there I discovered a sinful spread of luscious cakes and tarts, inviting me to indulge. The lackluster menu never had me salivating, but choosing from *le chariot* did.

I took my time and finally selected a healthy-sized wedge of *coup de soleil*, a wild strawberry *pâte sablée* tart topped with caramelized custard crème (*crème mousseline*). I've learned never to pass up a pastry made with *fraise de bois* during their spring season. The French don't irreverently throw around the term *fraises de bois*—it's reserved for the wild, handpicked variety. They are tiny and sweet, with the purest strawberry taste.

*Le chariot*'s other enticing options included a divine chocolate ganache and a creative clementine tart. There were also less frilly options like muffins, scones, *financiers*, and *madeleines*. The teas complement the pastries perfectly—my *coup de soleil* was extra-extravagant with a cup of South African *thé rouge*, a non-caffeinated, perfumed red tea.

This is definitely a different experience from my typical brioche-on-the-go, but in the end, I am a convert. The fancy, fussy Mariage Frères is fun for a change.

### ✦ ✦ ✦ Additional Locations ✦ ✦ ✦

13, RUE DES GRANDS-AUGUSTINS, 6TH ARR.

Telephone 01 40 51 82 50 ✦ Métro ODÉON

Boutique EVERY DAY 10:30AM to 7:30PM ✦ Tea Salon EVERY DAY NOON to 7PM

260, RUE FAUBOURG SAINT-HONORÉ, 8TH ARR.

Telephone 01 46 22 18 54 ✦ Métro TERNES

Boutique EVERY DAY 10:30AM to 7:30PM ✦ Tea Salon EVERY DAY NOON to 7PM

# Pozzetto

39 RUE DU ROI DE SICILE, 4TH ARR.

Telephone ✦ 01 42 77 08 64

Métro ✦ HÔTEL DE VILLE

Open DAILY NOON to 10:30PM

WHEN THE WEATHER TURNS WARM, I SWAP PASTRIES FOR ICE CREAM. NOTHING IS MORE SATISFYING THAN AN oversized, dripping cone on a hot day. Parisians have a love affair with *glace*, too—namely Berthillon on the Ile Saint-Louis, Paris' ice cream mecca. There's no doubt Berthilion's ice cream is delicious, but on a summer day, after waiting in line for forty-five minutes, the ping-pong-ball-size scoops are simply not worth the effort.

For a nearby alternative without the lines, try Pozzetto. "Little well" in Italian, *pozzetto* is also the word for the sunken metal pots that store the ice cream. According to Pozzetto ice cream-maker Mauro, this traditional Italian method maintains a consistent temperature, conserving the *gelato*'s delicate flavors and consistency though it doesn't have the marketing advantage of showcasing creamy mounds in a glass-covered display case. After tasting his handiwork, I'll take Mauro's word for it. Pozzetto's flavors change daily and are seasonal, depending on what's fresh at the market. Try lemon, white peach, or watermelon in the summer, and pear or fig in the fall. Each batch is made every morning. Chocolate lovers should try Pozzetto's specialty *gianduja Torinese*, chocolate with hazelnuts from Turin. Other good picks include pistachio, *café Costadoro*, or my favorite, *yogurt magro*, made from barely sweetened fresh yogurt.

# Les Ruchers du Roy

THE CULTIVATION OF HONEY IS AN ART IN FRANCE, AND *L'APICULTURE* (BEEKEEPING) IS CONSIDERED A *MÉTIER artisanal*, the much-lauded classification given to tradition-based crafts practiced by individual producers. Boutique Les Ruchers du Roy caters to the French zeal for all things honey-related, selling more than fifty pure varieties, from *miel d'acacia*, a mild, classic-flavored variety, to *miel au chataignier*, a dark, amber-colored, and richly flavored honey.

The shop also sells honey-based condiments, and honey-based products like candies, soaps, and a delicious *pain d'épices* made with 25% honey. The honeys are classified as single flower, mixed flower, or regional honeys. (For those who need a honey primer, the nectar collected by the bees flavors the honey, thus its color and taste is greatly influenced by the bee's environment.)

The French use honey liberally for cooking and baking and are serious honey evangelists who sing the praises of its purported medicinal properties. Just tell the shopkeeper what you want to use the honey for—marinating poultry or sweetening chamomile tea—and she will make a recommendation. You can also consult her on its medicinal properties. She will tell you which honey aids in digestion (white heather or clementine tree honey), relaxes the senses (maritime lavender), or increases circulation (chestnut tree honey). If you are having trouble choosing, her rule of thumb—the darker the honey, the stronger its flavor—helps in the selection.

You can buy honey directly from the producer at most of Paris' outdoor street markets. Talk to him/her about the *métier* to get firsthand information on each *parfum*. If you don't have the opportunity to visit a market, go to Les Ruchers du Roy, a good choice for exploring the world of honey.

### ✦ ✦ ✦ Additional Locations ✦ ✦ ✦

47, RUE DU CHERCHE-MIDI, 6TH ARR.
Telephone 01 45 44 19 85 ✦ Métro RENNES or SÈVRES-BABYLONE
Open MONDAY through SATURDAY 10:30AM to 2:00PM
and 2:30PM to 7:30PM ✦ Closed SUNDAY

17 RUE VIGNON, 8TH ARR.
Telephone 01 49 24 08 27 ✦ Métro MADELEINE
Open MONDAY through FRIDAY 10AM to 7:30PM
SATURDAY 10AM to 8PM ✦ Closed SUNDAY

# Sacha Finkelsztajn

27, RUE DES ROSIERS, 4<sup>TH</sup> ARR.

*Telephone* ✦ 01 42 72 78 91

*Métro* ✦ SAINT-PAUL

*Open* WEDNESDAY *through* MONDAY 10AM *to* 7PM ✦ *Closed* TUESDAY

SACHA FINKELSZTAJN IS A MARAIS INSTITUTION, OPENING IN 1946 JUST AS PARIS' JEWISH QUARTER WAS RETURNING to life after World War II. Of the Yiddish Central European and Russian specialties, recipes that current owner Sacha Finkelsztajn's grandparents brought from Poland when they founded the shop, I can't resist the *vatrouchka*, a cheesecake, and the Reine de Saba, a chocolate cake. Among the several varieties of cheesecake, the lemon has more punch than the plain or other fruit varieties. Finkelsztajn specifies that her Polish cheesecake is different from American and French versions. She is right—her recipe is extraordinarily moist and its texture resembles a flan more than a cake. It is not nearly as rich as American cheesecake, and less "cake-like" than the French *gâteau au fromage*, made with *fromage blanc*. The Reine de Saba tastes like a superior brownie, impossibly dense and chocolaty yet light

PLETZEL
Oignons Pavot
1 €uro 70
Piece

and airy at the same time. The cakes are giant sheet cakes; the servers cut squares according to how much you want. Be careful, prices add up quickly.

The sweets are delicious here, but savory Eastern European pies, spreads, and delicatessen items are Finkelsztajn's specialty. There are several cramped tables for eating on the spot. Most people take food to go, to eat while window-shopping.

What started as a neighborhood shop serving the Jewish community now attracts fans from all over Paris, especially on Sundays when Parisians stroll around the neighborhood, shopping in its boutiques when the rest of the city is closed.

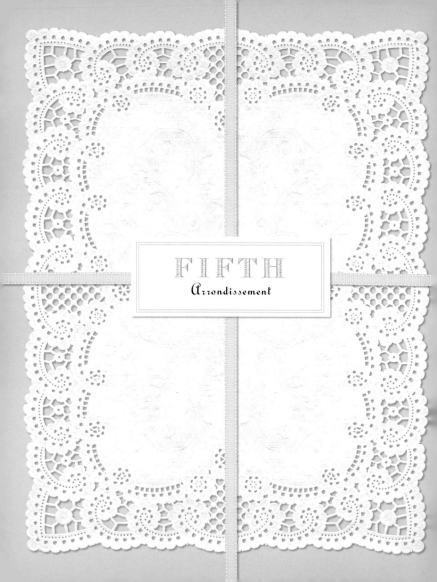

# FIFTH
### Arrondissement

# Boulangerie Bruno Solques

243, RUE SAINT-JACQUES, 5ᵀᴴ ARR.

*Telephone* ✦ 01 43 54 62 33

*Métro* ✦ LUXEMBOURG

*Open* MONDAY *through* FRIDAY 6:30AM *to* 8PM

**B**OULANGER SOLQUES' UNIQUE BREADS AND TARTS REFLECT HIS *GOÛT PERSONEL*, HIS OWN TASTE—THE TREATS HE enjoys making and eating. Solques steers clear of traditional goodies such as *palmiers* and *madeleines*, and instead focuses on unusual options like the *tourte aux épinards*, a *sablé* crust sandwiching a sweet spinach and raisin filling, with a dusting of powdered sugar (originally a Niçoise recipe made with Swiss chard). He has no interest in picture-perfect pastries; his free-form tarts of squashed berries on

a lopsided shell are charming and delicious. They may not appeal to everyone, but those who like his creations are devoted.

Solques started his own shop in 2001 to have artistic freedom and he relies on this appreciative clientele who enjoy his style. "I could make a traditional baguette that five out of ten people would like, or I can make my *pain au levain*, a particular taste that one out of ten people likes," he says. This way, Solques makes extremely limited quantities, with no waste. Indeed, arrive at the end of the day and most baskets are empty, with only a few loaves, and even fewer sweets, remaining.

Other favorites include the *fleur d'orange brioche*, satisfying but not heavy, and rolls made from croissant dough and filled with fruit or chocolate—beloved snack of the kids from the school across the street.

# Damman's

1, RUE GRANDE DEGRÉS, 5TH ARR.

Telephone ✦ 01 43 29 15 10

Métro ✦ MAUBERT-MUTUALITÉ

Open TUESDAY through SUNDAY NOON to 11PM ✦ Closed MONDAY

WHEN THE LINES ARE TOO LONG FOR A CONE ON ILE SAINT-LOUIS, WALK ACROSS THE BRIDGE TO THE FIFTH arrondissement and sample Damman's. On the river just across from Notre Dame, this largely undiscovered shop's quality is on par with Berthilion and other island favorites. Flavors are creative and fresh. The *yaourt Bulgare* (Bulgarian yogurt) is my favorite in Paris; its fermentation process gives it a particular, tangy, and delicious taste. Lucky for me, they sell tubs to go, complete with Styrofoam boxes for melt-free transport.

# Gelati d'Alberto

45, RUE MOUFFETARD, 5ᵀᴴ ARR.

*Telephone* + 01 43 37 88 07

*Métro* + PLACE MONGE

Open EVERY DAY NOON to MIDNIGHT (APRIL through AUGUST), TUESDAY
through SUNDAY 12:30PM to MIDNIGHT (SEPTEMBER through DECEMBER)

Closed JANUARY, FEBRUARY, MARCH

FRUIT SORBETS ARE THIS *GELATERIA*'S SPECIALTY, MADE FROM RECIPES THAT ITALIAN OWNER AND ICE CREAM MAKER Alberto learned in his native Parma. A scoop of melon tastes like biting into the juiciest, ripest fruit you've ever eaten. *Rose d'orient* is delicate and lightly perfumed. Yogurt sells like crazy in the summer, and is best paired with a sorbet. Whimsical flavors like cookies and Nutella are also fun to try.

### + + + Additional Location + + +

12, RUE DES LOMBARDS, 4ᵀᴴ ARR.

*Telephone* 01 77 11 44 55 + *Métro* CHÂTELET

Open DAILY NOON to 12:30AM (APRIL through AUGUST), TUESDAY through
SUNDAY 12:30PM to MIDNIGHT (SEPTEMBER through OCTOBER)

Closed NOVEMBER through MARCH

# Kayser

8, RUE MONGE, 5TH ARR.

*Telephone* ◆ 01 44 07 01 42

*Métro* ◆ MAUBERT-MUTUALIÉ

*Open* WEDNESDAY *through* MONDAY 7AM *to* 8:30 PM

ERIC KAYSER, BOULANGER EXTRAORDINAIRE, IS A HOUSE-HOLD PARIS NAME KNOWN FOR HIS EXCELLENT BREADS. His eleven shops around the city (and others in France and around the world) sell every imaginable variety and combination of grain, nut, cheese, or fruit.

The impressive bread selection overshadows the sweet counter, but pastries are *pas mal* (not bad) either. And, like everything else *chez* Kayser, they are certainly bold—in selection and size. More than twenty-five types of *viennoiserie* include cakes, financiers, brioches, and *cannelés,* the bordelais specialty. Oversized square tarts are available in countless flavors, varying by shop. Try the *Périgourdin*, a hazelnut biscuit crust with ganache, coffee mousse, and nutty nougatine filling, or the *Sangra*, with wild strawberry and lime mousse. For chocolate lovers, the all-chocolate mousse and cream *noir désir* is about as good as it gets. Kayser's pastries aren't delicate—their thick heft allows you to sink your teeth in and enjoy.

Savory items make a statement too—huge slices of quiche, extra large *fougasse*, or overstuffed sandwiches of brie and veggies on olive bread make a more-than-satisfying lunch. There are ten additional locations throughout Paris.

# La Mosquée

39, RUE GEOFFROY ST.-HILAIRE, 5TH ARR.

*Telephone* ✦ 01 43 31 38 20

*Métro* ✦ CENSIER-DAUBENTON or JUSSIEU

*Open* DAILY 9AM to MIDNIGHT

FRANCE'S OLDEST MOSQUE SEEMS LIKE AN UNLIKELY PLACE TO RELAX WITH A MINT TEA AND SAVOR A MOROCCAN PASTRY, but it is an experience not to be missed. The Moorish atmosphere is lively and transporting; the pastries are authentic and delicious.

Select your sweets at the counter, choosing from *cornes de gazelles*, the classic horn-shaped, almond paste-filled biscuits, baklava, honey-soaked phyllo with cashews, or my favorite—gooey semolina cakes drenched in honey with a hint of *fleur d'oranger*. There are countless varieties to decipher—most all variations on the nut/honey/pastry theme. It's a matter of deciding on cashews, almonds, hazelnuts, or pistachios, honey or powdered sugar, semolina or phyllo, sugar-topped or not.

After assembling a pastry plate, settle into a blue-tiled table on the courtyard patio or head inside to one of the frescoed tearooms infused with the aroma of hookahs. Take a steaming glass of sweet mint tea from a waiter passing trays with a fresh, hot supply. Gorge yourself on the sticky snacks, wash it down with the tea, and enjoy the atmosphere. The Mosque also has a restaurant featuring Moroccan tajines and couscous specialties and a *hammam*, or bath, that is popular among young Parisians. Bathing times are segregated, so call ahead for up-to-date hours.

# Mouff' Tartes

53, RUE MOUFFETARD, 5TH ARR.

Telephone ✦ 01 43 37 21 89

Métro ✦ PLACE MONGE

Open TUESDAY through SUNDAY NOON to 9:30PM

ON THE TOURISTY RUE MOUFFETARD, THIS EXCELLENT TART SPECIALIST IS A GREAT FIND. YOU CAN'T MISS THE SHOP window's rows of homemade sweet and savory filled pies—apricot pistachio, chocolate, fig, or eggplant feta, chicken vegetable, or spinach, just to name a few. Owner Yafeh bakes the *sucrées* (sweet) while his sister makes the *salées* (savory), and each have a repertoire of fifteen varieties. Specialties such as caramelized onion and Comté cheese, and fig and chèvre are original house recipes. Yafeh's lemon meringue tart is so over-the-top that he only makes it for the weekend crowd (when customers are more willing to indulge). It's too *costaude* ("hefty") for the week, he says.

An avid cook who learned from his mother, Yafeh gave up his architecture career three years ago to start Mouff' Tartes with her special crust recipe. Dining in or taking out, the quiches make a delicious bargain meal, followed by dessert, of course. Full tarts serving six or eight are available for order a day in advance.

# Piccadis Boulangerie-Pâtisserie

8, RUE GAY LUSSAC, 5TH ARR.

Telephone ✦ 01 43 54 31 69

Métro ✦ LUXEMBOURG

Open MONDAY through FRIDAY 7:15AM to 8:15PM

SATURDAY 8AM to 7:45PM ✦ Closed SUNDAY

FAT RIBBONS OF MULTICOLORED MARSHMALLOWS ARE STACKED IN PICCADIS' WINDOW, ACCOMPANIED BY AN intriguing tiny handwritten sign claiming, *"La véritable guimauve de Paris"* ("the genuine Paris marshmallow"). No one knows how or when this traditional *boulangerie*, started in 1864, first brought marshmallows to the neighborhood, but the current owners have preserved their stellar reputation, supplying favorites like chocolate, vanilla, lemon, raspberry, and cherry to their loyal customers. *Les guimauves* are a *"produit d'antan"* (an old-fashioned treat), says the owner. It's usually grandparents who bring in their offspring for a taste. That must explain why coffee and orange, decidedly grown-up flavors, are the first to sell out on weekends.

Other best sellers include homey goodies like *madeleines*, croissants, and *gâteau de riz*, a chewy rice pudding cake. The fruit tarts are excellent, as in the *pavé citron*, lemon curd sandwiched in slices of sponge cake.

Piccadis' specialty breads include the *batard au levain* (a hand-kneaded baguette) and the *mignonnette* (a tomato confit and olive breadstick) that are baked fresh several times a day to keep up with demand.

# SIXTH
*Arrondissement*

# L'Artisan de Saveurs

72, RUE DU CHERCHE-MIDI, 6ᵀᴴ ARR.

Telephone ✦ 01 42 22 46 64

Métro ✦ VANEAU OR RENNES

Open THURSDAY through TUESDAY NOON to 6:30PM ✦ Closed WEDNESDAY

HARD TO BELIEVE I HAD BEEN IN PARIS FOR ALMOST THREE YEARS BEFORE DISCOVERING MY DREAM DESSERT —*pain de Gênes*, a rich almond butter cake. It was the menu's lemony description of *pain de Gênes au citron* that got my attention. I didn't expect two almond-sprinkled cake triangles with a luscious slathering of lemon cream in between, drizzled with berry *coulis*, perfectly poised on a large white platter. I immediately knew I was in good hands at L'Artisan de Saveurs. Desserts are serious here, an intriguing mix of classic and inventive creations. Kumquat preserves add a kick to a bitter chocolate tart. The pear *charlotte* is spiced up with *pain d'épices*. A *blanc manger*, usually an almond and cream custard, is updated with coconut and exotic fruits. There are also scones and platters of mini macarons. *Pain d'épices* slices are served with loads of butter and honey on the side. The tea is serious too, with more than fifty types from which to choose.

# La Bonbonnière de Buci

12, RUE DE BUCI, 6TH ARR.

*Telephone* ✦ 01 43 26 97 13

*Métro* ✦ MABILLON

*Open* DAILY 8AM to 9PM

IF *MILLEFEUILLE* IS YOUR *PÂTISSERIE PREFÈRÉE*, LA BONBONN-IERE DE BUCI IS FOR YOU. ITS NAME MEANS "CANDYBOX," BUT this *pâtisserie* specializes in *millefeuille*, offering ten different varieties, classics plus original creations such as pear caramel, praline, kirsch, Grand Marnier, and strawberry with whipped cream.

Somehow when I am on Paris' Left Bank, I always seem to end up here, at the intersection of rue de Buci and rue de Seine. This busy pedestrian thoroughfare, the heart of the sixth arrondissement, is chock full of crowded cafés, *boulangeries*, and food *traiteurs*. In the midst of it all, is this decidedly untrendy, hole-in-the-wall *pâtisserie*.

La Bonbonniere de Buci may not have the best-looking shop or the best-dressed pastries, but *pâtissier* Pierre Marandon prides himself on using only fresh fruit for his *millefeuille* and other pastries. He also claims to make Paris' best *palmiers*, those ubiquitous "elephant ears" drenched in butter and sugar and baked to a crisp. Marandon's are extra buttery and flaky, deserving of his self-proclaimed, super-lative title.

Supplying croissants to many of the neighborhood cafés, La Bonbon-nière de Buci has mastered the buttery *viennoiserie*. An upstairs *salon de thé* with tables (and a restroom) also makes this a convenient stop.

# The Croissant

THE NOW UBIQUITOUS CROISSANT IS A RELATIVE NEWCOMER TO THE FRENCH BREAKFAST TABLE, NOT APPEARING IN ITS CURRENT FORM UNTIL THE EARLY TWENTIETH CENTURY. YET FEW SPECIALTIES HAVE COME TO SYMBOLIZE FRANCE, CAPTURING THE APPETITES OF BOTH FOREIGNERS AND NATIONALS, LIKE THE CROISSANT. TO WHAT DOES IT OWE ITS ALLURE?

The croissant's respected status can most likely be explained by its complex taste and delicate consistency, its labor-intensive fabrication, and the expertise required to make it. Its buttery layers demand a light touch, making a really good croissant a treasure to come by. (Adding to its fascination and "Frenchness," it's practically impossible to find a "real" one outside of France.)

Croissant dough is made of flour, butter, sugar, yeast, and a pinch of salt, with sometimes a touch of milk or egg to create its golden hue. High-quality butter is of utmost importance, *boulangers* say. Thus the labeling, croissant *au beurre*, made with pure butter, or croissant *ordinaire*, with margarine.

The dough is rolled and layered in sheets, then cut into triangles, then rolled into its "crescent" form. When baked, its flaky layers rise, it puffs, and its exterior turns a golden brown.

Of course, individual tastes vary, but most connoisseurs agree that the perfect croissant should be flaky and light, not too dense or doughy. The bread should be slightly sweet and balanced with a salty tinge. It should be buttery and rich without being greasy, and shouldn't leave an oily film on your fingers or tongue.

The croissant's sibling, the *pain au chocolat*, is favored by children as an after-school snack. It's made from the same pastry dough, only it's folded into a rectangle around two (or one, in inferior versions) sticks of chocolate. The *pain aux raisins* can be a different species altogether, frequently made from brioche dough, which renders it chewier and less flakey. It is spiraled into a snail shape, and layered with *crème pâtissiere* and raisins.

# Christian Constant

37, RUE D'ASSAS, 6<sup>TH</sup> ARR.

Telephone • 01 53 63 15 15

Métro • RENNES

Open MONDAY through FRIDAY 9:30AM to 8:30PM

SATURDAY and SUNDAY 9AM to 8PM

CHRISTIAN CONSTANT SPECIALIZES IN CHOCOLATE. IN HIS BOOK ON THE SUBJECT, HIS FRIEND SONIA RYKIEL WRITES in the prologue, "I love chocolates that are crazy, bizarre, and unusual." It is no wonder that Rykiel is a fan of Constant's breed—chocolates with a strong personality.

Ganaches are flavored with cardamon, frangipani flowers, or Chinese ginger, to name a few. Constant's most revered *pâtisserie* is his basic chocolate tart, simply pure chocolate filling a *sablé* crust. Other specialties include the *fleurs de Chine*, flaky pastry layered with bitter chocolate mousse and jasmine green tea cream. The *soleil noir*'s chocolate mousse is perfumed with cinnamon, while the *Pont Royal* features hazelnut cream and kirsch-soaked biscuits.

# Le Confiturier

20, RUE CHERCHE-MIDI, 6TH ARR.

*Telephone* ◆ 01 45 49 33 64

*Métro* ◆ SÈVRES-BABYLONE or SAINT-SULPICE

*Open* TUESDAY *through* SATURDAY 8AM to 7PM

*Closed* SUNDAY *and* MONDAY

I LOVE THE FRENCH *PETIT DÉJEUNER*. SOMETIMES ON WEEK-ENDS, I'LL RUSH HOME WITH A WARM BAGUETTE FROM THE *boulangerie* and slather it with butter and homemade jams found in Paris' outdoor markets. Combined with a *café crème*, it is the ultimate indulgence. Part of the fun is the presentation: the *petit pots* of jams, the *café au lait* bowls, the sugar cubes, and steaming milk. I'd searched cafés endlessly for this ideal, and began to think it was an outdated concept, found only in homey, countryside B&Bs and fancy hotels…until I found Le Confiturier.

Meaning "jam maker/seller," Le Confiturier's café/*salon de thé* is one of the few spots in Paris where you can have a thick slab of brioche, served with jams and butter, at any time of day. For breakfast, have it with coffee and juice. Later in the

day, try it with eggs or *fromage blanc* and honey. Don't miss other delicacies like the *cannellé*, *financiers*, *tartelette au citron*, or *tartelette aux pommes*. Lunch offers hearty salads, cheese, and *charcuterie* plates, or *tartines* (gourmet open-faced sandwiches).

Le Confiturier's French farmhouse feel is kitch-free, with a clean design blending caramel-colored, rough-hewn beams and warm, exposed-stone walls. The service is among the most efficient I've seen for this sort of leisurely place.

# Café, Café crème, or Café au lait?

ANY CAFÉ-GOERS HAVE UNHAPPILY SLURPED DOWN A COFFEE THAT DIDN'T TURN OUT TO BE WHAT THEY THOUGHT THEY WERE ORDERING, NOT WANTING TO CALL ATTENTION TO THEIR IGNORANCE BUT DESPERATELY WONDERING HOW TO GET IT RIGHT THE NEXT TIME. HOW COULD SOMETHING AS BASIC AS COFFEE BE SO DISCOURAGINGLY MYSTIFYING?

It's confusing because there is little standard beyond the basic *café*. Order it and you'll get an espresso (also called an *express*)—that much is certain. A *café crème* (or simply "*un crème*" in waiter-speak) will get you a coffee with milk, but the amount of milk can vary from a few drops to a very light colored cup (usually the former). You'll rarely hear a French person order a *café au lait*—they'll call it a *crème*—and in general they'll never order one after 11 a.m. Normally the milk is added warm, but sometimes you'll be served a small pitcher of milk on the side. If your *crème* isn't light enough for you, don't be afraid to ask for "*un peu plus du lait*" and the server will bring you more to add. That's perfectly acceptable, especially at breakfast time. There's no formula, so don't be timid.

If you want a weaker cup, order a *café Americain* or *allongé* and the server will add hot water to an espresso, watering it down. It's usually possible to order a *décaféiné (un déca)*, but not all cafés offer it.

Tea drinkers, order *un thé*, thé *au lait* (with milk), or *une infusion*, herbal tea.

When in France, don't even think about ordering a cappuccino, even if you see it on the menu. They are usually not very good—save it for Italy!

# Les Deux Magots

6, PLACE SAINT-GERMAIN-DES-PRÉS, 6TH ARR.

Telephone ✦ 01 45 48 55 25

Métro ✦ SAINT-GERMAIN-DES-PRÉS

Open EVERY DAY 7:30PM to 12:30AM

LES DEUX MAGOTS IS WELL KNOWN FOR ITS HISTORY AS A PRESTIGIOUS LITERARY HANGOUT, NOT FOR ITS FOOD. SO who would've guessed that this famous café has delicious desserts? Go and enjoy the legendary atmosphere over coffee and a creamy, rich dark chocolate mousse or warm *tarte Tatin* with vanilla ice cream.

I can vouch that reviews of mediocre, overpriced food do not apply to the desserts, all but one expertly-made by La Petit Marquise, a highly regarded seventh arrondissement *pâtisserie*. (The exception is Pierre Hermé's *Ispahan*, his flashy cream-filled raspberry *macaron*). Ask to see the dessert menu and a *serveuse* arrives at your table with a loaded tray, presenting lemon, *mirabelle*, or apricot pistachio tarts, chocolate *entremets*, a raspberry vanilla cream cake, a *Mont Blanc*, or chocolate éclair, among others. No need to save your appetite for the corner *pâtisserie*—all are excellent.

Coffee is served by the pot, with milk on the side, so you may adjust the crème to your palate. The infusion *à la menthe*, fresh mint leaves steeped in hot water and served with an elegant strainer, is a refreshing treat. A light menu is available all day with savory snacks, and a dinner menu is available from 7 to 11 p.m.

Les Deux Magots' ambiance is lively and fun, appreciated by Parisians and tourists alike. A Sunday afternoon finds tables of elderly French couples reading, college-aged tourists chattering, and local families with children crammed into red leather banquettes. The classic character spills onto the terrace in season, where café-goers admire the church of Saint-Germain-des-Prés *en face*, while they sip champagne or dip into a meringue-coated *tarte au citron*, and watch the world go by.

Les Deux Magots has seen scores of famous patrons since it was founded in 1884, including Guillaume Apollinaire, Oscar Wilde, André Breton, and Max Ernst. And in case you are wondering about the name's origin—it comes from the previous tenant, a boutique whose only other remnants are two Asian statues on the corner wall.

# Gerard Mulot

76, RUE DE SEINE, 6TH ARR.

Telephone ✦ 01 43 26 85 77

Métro ✦ ODEON or MABILLON

Open DAILY 6:45AM to 8PM

GERARD MULOT STANDS OUT AS ONE OF PARIS' BEST-KNOWN AND MOST LOVED "NEIGHBORHOOD" *PÂTISSIERS*, EVEN FOR those who live far from his St.-Germain shop. Parisians feel an intimacy, a connection to his mouth-watering pastries, elicited by years of Sunday morning croissants or special celebrations marked by a Mulot cake. "*Un grand classique,*" Parisians from all over the city exclaim about this *pâtissier*, who for twenty-five years has catered to their indulgences with perfected expertise and always-delicious sweets.

Not surprisingly, there is little consensus on Mulot's "best" creations. Some say the *macarons* (orange ginger, passion fruit basil, orange cinnamon, or simple chocolate, to name a few flavors) are incomparable. Many claim his croissant is perfection. Others line up for slices of cherry *clafoutis* or peach tart from baking sheets stacked on the counter. Sentiments run strong for his classic cakes. But there is unanimous awe over the extensive selection, and the quality of everything.

Some of the more original specialties include the *cannelier*, cinnamon cream sandwiched by two spiced cake biscuits, the nougat *millefeuille*, and the *ardéchois*, a winter favorite of chestnut mousse with chestnut chunks, chocolate biscuit soaked in whiskey, with vanilla *crème anglaise*. And of course, Mulot's classics are always in style—the *Saint Honoré*, the *Paris-Brest* or the *Opéra*. Mulot also has an excellent savory selection of salads and tarts—perfect for a picnic in the Luxembourg Gardens up the street.

### ✦ ✦ ✦ Additional Location ✦ ✦ ✦

93, RUE DE LA GLACIÈRE, 13TH ARR.

Telephone 01 45 81 39 09 ✦ Métro GLACIÈRE

Open TUESDAY through FRIDAY 10AM to 7:30PM, SATURDAY and SUNDAY
9:30AM to 7:30PM ✦ Closed MONDAY

# Jean Charles Rochoux

16, RUE D'ASSAS, 6TH ARR.

Telephone ✦ 01 42 84 29 45

Métro ✦ RENNES

Open TUESDAY through SATURDAY 10:30AM to 7:30PM

MONDAY 2:30PM to 7:30PM ✦ Closed SUNDAY

JEAN CHARLES ROCHOUX IS NOT A FANCY, BIG-NAME *CHOCOLAT-IER*, YET LOCALS KNOW THAT HIS TINY, NON-DESCRIPT SHOP turns out some of Paris' best chocolate. Established in 2004, he has recently gained much-deserved recognition for his creative, high-quality products like the specialty *Durango*, caramelized almonds coated with chocolate praline. My favorite is the *mousse marron*, chocolate-covered, lightly whipped chestnut cream. Other unique choices include the *Loja*, a rose-flavored ganache and the *Louise*, chocolate infused with basil. All chocolate is made in the basement *laboratoire* and is available only in the shop.

# Pâtisserie Sadaharu Aoki

35, RUE VAUGIRARD, 6TH ARR.

Telephone ✦ 01 45 44 48 90

Métro ✦ RENNES

Open MONDAY through SATURDAY 11AM to 7PM, SUNDAY 11AM to 6PM

THE MINIMALIST *PÂTISSERIE* SADAHARU AOKI, TUCKED IN A NARROW STOREFRONT DOWN THE STREET FROM LUXEMbourg Gardens, creates what may be Paris' most exquisite pastries. Bursting with color, meticulously formed into geometric perfection, each *millefeuille*, éclair, and *tarte* is a specimen of Japanese high art meeting the classic French interpretation. Precisely aligned in their glass-topped case, there's not much else in the shop, save two tiny tables for eating *sur place*, to distract you from admiring them.

*Pâtissier* Sadaharu Aoki has succeeded in winning over Parisians to his fusion style, starting with their beloved *millefeuille*. He gently whips *mâcha* (green tea powder) into pastry cream, creating the *millefeuille mâcha*, one of his most popular. Other fusion specialties include the *Duomo Mâcha Azuki*, delicate green *mâcha* pastry cream wrapped around a *mâcha macaron*, *feuilleté* pastry, and Japanese sweet red bean paste. Aoki uses the *mâcha* cream liberally, along with other Asian flavors such as sesame, to infuse a Japanese accent into his creations.

All of Aoki's pastries share his signature delicacy: Tastes reveal themselves one layer at a time, like slicing a cross section and discovering a vivid cache of colors and textures. The *citron praliné* is a soft mound of lemon and white chocolate cream over a lemon *macaron* and praline *feuilleté* pastry. His chocolate creations are smooth, perfect balances of milk and dark chocolate, layers of meringue sponge cake, praline cream, and sometimes liqueurs.

Aoki's pastries are featured at upscale Paris tea salons, including Maison de la Chine, an idyllic oasis around the corner on rue Bonaparte, and Japanese tea salon Toraya in the first arrondissement.

### ✦ ✦ ✦ Additional Locations ✦ ✦ ✦

56, BOULEVARD PORT-ROYAL, 5TH ARR.
Telephone 01 45 35 36 80 ✦ Métro LES GOBELINS
Open MONDAY through FRIDAY 8AM to 7:30PM,
SATURDAY 9AM to 7:30PM ✦ Closed SUNDAY

✦

BOUTIQUE LAFAYETTE GOURMET
40, BOULEVARD HAUSSMANN, 9TH ARR.
Métro ✦ HAVRE-CAUMARTIN
Open MONDAY through SATURDAY 9:30AM to 7:30PM,
THURSDAY until 9PM ✦ Closed SUNDAY

# Patrick Roger Chocolatier

108, BOULEVARD SAINT-GERMAIN, 6ᵀᴴ ARR.

Telephone ✦ 01 43 29 38 42

Métro ✦ CLUNY LA SORBONNE

Open TUESDAY through SATURDAY 10:30AM to 7:30PM

PATRICK ROGER HAS A REPUTATION AS THE WILD CHILD OF THE CHOCOLATE WORLD. HE TELLS STORIES OF HIS YOUNGER days of scholastic ennui and touring France by motorcycle, before discovering his *métier* as a *chocolatier*, opening his first shop ten years ago in the village of Sceaux, and being selected *Meilleur Ouvrier de France* in 2000. Today, his tourist-jammed, internationally-

renowned shop testifies to his success and mastery of the craft of chocolate-making. Roger's bold approach is evident in his creative flavors and products. Not least of Roger's spirited statements are shop window displays—recently showcasing mod design valentines next to giant penguins sculpted from 80-kg. solid chocolate blocks. Not-to-miss chocolates include the award-winning *désir*, a crunchy chocolate praline, or the less conservative *Beijing*, powerfully flavored with chunks of root ginger. Caramel with lime or pear and honey, and almond and chocolate "married" with chestnut round out Roger's inspired, unusual selection.

### ✦ ✦ ✦ Additional Location ✦ ✦ ✦

45, AVENUE VICTOR HUGO, 16TH ARR.

Telephone ✦ 01 45 01 66 71

Métro ✦ VICTOR HUGO or KLÉBER

MONDAY through FRIDAY 11AM to 7:30PM,

Open SATURDAY 10:30AM to 7:30PM ✦ Closed SUNDAY

# Pierre Hermé Paris

72, RUE BONAPARTE, 6TH ARR.

Telephone ✦ 01 43 54 47 77

Métro ✦ SAINT-SULPICE

Open TUESDAY through FRIDAY 10AM to 7PM,
SATURDAY 10AM to 7:30PM ✦ Closed SUNDAY

PIERRE HERMÉ IS ONE OF THE BIGGEST NAMES IN FRENCH PASTRIES, WELL KNOWN FOR HIS GLOSSY EPONYMOUS cookbook and artistic, inventive approach to his craft. Only a tiny, barely-visible sign identifies his closet-sized shop, but it is still frequently overrun by Parisians and "in-the-know" tourists clamoring for a peak at his sumptuous works of art—pastries that are at once intricate and fanciful.

The trademarked *2000 feuilles* lives up to the hype with seemingly 2,000 flaky layers of caramelized, paper-thin pastry and praline mousse cream. Cutting into the delicate, pale green sphere of *le désir* reveals beautiful striped layers of strawberry banana jam, lemon cream, and soft lemon cake grounded on *sablé* crust.

Hermé's pastries are not for eating-on-the-go. They are elaborate and even more elaborately packaged. *Macarons*, with a choice of intriguing, exotic flavors, are among the more accessible choices. Not usually a huge fan of *macarons*, I melt over Hermé's light, springy outer cakes yielding to a creamy, intensely flavorful interior. Olive oil and vanilla, one of Hermé's signatures, is a delicate and precise balance of the two flavors. Praline and hazelnut white truffle are almost as perfect. All over Paris, in fact, the mundane sandwich cookie has become a sophisticate, its ingredients able somehow to perfectly capture the essence of a variety of flavors. Big-name *pâtisseries artisanales* try to outdo one another with increasingly unusual, even bizarre flavors. But Pierre Hermé's are among the best.

### ✦ ✦ ✦ Additional Location ✦ ✦ ✦

185, RUE DE VAUGIRARD, 15TH ARR.

Telephone 01 47 83 89 96 ✦ Métro PASTEUR or VOLONTAIRES

Open TUESDAY and WEDNESDAY 10AM to 7PM, THURSDAY through
SATURDAY 10AM to 7:30PM, SUNDAY 10AM to 6PM ✦ Closed MONDAY

# Poilâne

8, RUE DU CHERCHE-MIDI, 6TH ARR.

Telephone ✦ 01 45 48 42 59

Métro ✦ SAINT-SULPICE or SÈVRES-BABYLONE

Open MONDAY through SATURDAY 7:15AM to 8:15PM ✦ Closed SUNDAY

FRANCE'S MOST FAMOUS BAKERY IS KNOWN FOR ITS EPONYMOUS SOURDOUGH LOAF, BUT SWEET LOVERS SHOULD TAKE note of Poilâne's butter cookies and apple tarts.

*Punitions* ("punishments"), the bite-sized, crunchy *sablés*, are impossible to resist, and I can't help stopping into Poilâne's St.-Germain-des-Prés shop for a taste whenever I'm passing by (there's usually a "help yourself" basket on the counter). The *tarte aux pommes* is truly special—a melt-in-your-mouth pastry crust topped with fresh, caramelized apple slices.

Poilâne has been a revered *boulangerie artisanale* since it was founded in 1932. Today, the company is run by the third generation of the Poilâne family, daughter Appolonia, who took over in 2002 at age seventeen after her parents died in a helicopter accident. She has maintained the *boulangerie*'s high standards and focus on consistent quality.

Poilâne's breads are so distinctive and delicious that loyal fans world-wide clamor to have them shipped to far-flung locations. Fortunately for them, the bread's crusty exterior and chewy interior lasts up to a week and renders it hardy enough for the voyage. *Punitions* can be shipped too, and last up to a month.

### ✦ ✦ ✦ Additional Location ✦ ✦ ✦

49, BOULEVARD DE GRENELLE, 15TH ARR.

Telephone ✦ 01 45 79 11 49

Métro ✦ DUPLEIX

Open TUESDAY through SUNDAY 7:15AM to 8:15PM ✦ Closed MONDAY

# SEVENTH
## Arrondissement

# Le Bac à Glace

109, RUE DE BAC, 7TH ARR.

Telephone ✦ 01 45 48 87 65

Métro ✦ SÈVRES-BABYLONE

Open MONDAY through SATURDAY 11AM to 7PM (SATURDAY 7:30PM)

Closed SUNDAY

WHEN AN ICE CREAM CRAVING HITS, LEFT BANK LOCALS HEAD TO LE BAC À GLACE. JUST BEHIND LE BON MARCHÉ department store, Le Bac à Glace is a real neighborhood ice cream shop, with a steady line of children to prove it. This *glacier artisanal* has been an after-school stop since 1982, offering all the usual favorites, plus *nouveau* combinations like apricot with ginger, rosemary peach, and honey pine nut. The chocolate sorbet with raspberries is popular, as is the coffee and caramel ice cream. The sign out front announces the flavor of the day, sure to be a fresh, seasonal sorbet.

If you recognize any of these flavors from the dessert menu at last night's restaurant, there's a good chance they came from Le Bac à Glace, as it supplies many restaurants and cafés around the city. Individuals can also buy tubs to take home.

The shop has a small traditional *salon de thé* and a few sidewalk tables. Or, take a cone to go and join the kids in the park down the street.

# Besnier Père et Fils

40, RUE DE BOURGOGNE, 7ᵀᴴ ARR.

*Telephone* ✦ 01 45 51 24 29

*Métro* ✦ VARENNE

*Open* MONDAY *through* FRIDAY 7AM *to* 8PM

*Closed* CLOSED SATURDAY *and* SUNDAY

SEVENTH-ARRONDISSEMENT NEIGHBORS-IN-THE-KNOW HEAD TO BESNIER PÈRE ET FILS FOR PASTRIES. YOU COULD EASILY walk past this nondescript shop without a glance—the limited selection is underwhelming—but excellent quality pastries, *viennoiserie*, chocolates, and breads are tucked inside. Try the *tarte figue pistache* or the *coup de soleil*, a *sablé* crust smothered with wine-marinated peaches and topped with lightly whipped orange cream. The *brioche chocolat*'s creamy chocolate interior is rich and much more satisfying than the usual *pépites*-filled variety, where chocolate bits are sprinkled throughout.

# Boulangerie-Pâtisserie P. P. Colas

178, RUE DE GRENELLE, 7<sup>TH</sup> ARR.

*Telephone* ◆ 01 45 51 06 35

*Métro* ◆ LA TOUR-MAUBOURG

*Open* MONDAY *through* FRIDAY 7:30AM *to* 8PM

*Closed* SATURDAY *and* SUNDAY

STOP INTO *BOULANGERIE-PÂTISSERIE* P.P. COLAS FOR ITS *PÂTISSERIE* OR *PAIN DU JOUR*, SEASONAL SPECIALTIES PRE-sented on the blackboard out front. A recent note—"*Les quetsches sont de retour*"—announced fresh tarts starring these sweet early autumn plums. Neighborhood favorite *quatre quart*, a yellow cake named for its four equal parts of sugar, flour, eggs, and butter, also is advertised, heralding the day's market-fresh fruit variety, often blueberry or raspberry.

Inside, a large selection of pastries, *viennoiserie*, and breads are crammed in a tiny space. The *financier* has a perfect crusty outside and a soft almond center. The *far Breton*, Brittany's famous prune cake, is moist and not too heavy. Little *pots* of *crème brûlée* and *mousse au chocolat* are lined up, alternating brown and cream colors. P.P. Colas' pink and green marzipan pigs will delight kids, as will *le patate*, a chocolate biscuit rolled in almond paste. Named for its unassuming likeness, this deep brown clunky mound of chocolate is surely one of Paris' most unappealing-looking sweets.

The *pain du jour* is also worth a taste. It is usually a unique creation, like the *marguerite*, a flower-shaped baguette.

# Debauve & Gallais

30, RUE DES SAINTS-PÈRES, 7TH ARR.

Telephone ✦ 01 45 48 54 67

Métro ✦ SAINT-GERMAIN-DES-PRÉS

Open MONDAY through SATURDAY 9:30AM to 6:30PM ✦ Closed SUNDAY

AS THE OLDEST *CHOCOLATIER* IN PARIS, DEBAUVE & GALLAIS HAS QUITE A REPUTATION TO UPHOLD. TASTE THEIR PRALINES and ganaches, and you'll agree they've been successful in maintaining two centuries of quality and tradition. Gourmand regulars stop by the shop two, sometimes three, times a week to pick up favorites like the *rucher*, a honey ganache, the *Babel*, a nut and *gianduja* mixture, or the *specialité rocher* of crunchy almond, praline, and hazelnut. While admiring the shop's splendidly restored original décor, they can commune with the spirits of many chocolate-lovers who stood at the beautiful crescent-shaped counter before them.

According to Debauve & Gallais lore, founder Sulpice Debauve prepared cocoa-based treats for Louis XVI and Marie Antoinette in his role as pharmacist to the Versailles court. After the revolution, he opened this original rue des Saint-Pères location and commissioned Napoleon's architects to create the stunning décor of a classical temple with a half-moon display counter.

One master *chocolatier* makes all Debauve & Gallais' chocolates, guaranteeing quality and consistency (and high prices).

### ✦✦✦ Additional Location ✦✦✦

33, RUE VIVIENNE, 2ND ARR.

Telephone 01 40 39 05 50 ✦ Métro BOURSE

Open MONDAY through SATURDAY 9AM to 7PM ✦ Closed SUNDAY

D&B opened this location near the Bourse in 1990, but the shop has housed a chocolatier since 1900 and also boasts original décor. The façade is not to be missed.

# Delicabar

LE BON MARCHÉ, 1ST FLOOR

26–38, RUE DE SÈVRES, 7TH ARR.

Telephone ✦ 01 42 22 10 12

Métro ✦ SÈVRES-BABYLONE

HOURS same as LE BON MARCHÉ: MONDAY through FRIDAY 9:30AM to 7PM

(THURSDAY until 9PM) SATURDAY 9:30AM to 8PM ✦ Closed SUNDAY

NESTLED IN THE FIRST-FLOOR WOMEN'S FASHION DEPARTMENT OF LE BON MARCHÉ, PARIS' MOST EXCLUSIVE *GRAND magasin*, this chic snack/lunch spot is a trendsetter in its own right. With a menu starring three ingredients—vegetables, fruits, and chocolate—pastry chef Sébastien Gaudard breaks traditional boundaries and invites diners to indulge "without thinking too hard about crossing the line between savory or sweet." Desserts carry equal weight on a cleverly arranged menu that mixes sugary and salty options, identifying them by color-coded print (mocha-colored for *sucré* or black for *salé*).

Pair a savory green vegetable consommé with a sweet soup of chocolate and stewed spiced apples. Indulge in a creamy *sabayon au chocolat* or rich *sabayon gratiné* with comté cheese and potatoes. Have two *tartelettes*, spinach followed by passion fruit.

Or try a *"fine-feuille,"* a take on the classic *millefeuille*, with two thin flaky pastry layers sandwiching smoked salmon and *fromage blanc* with herbs. Even *viennoiserie* crosses into savory territory. The traditional "elephant ears" *palmier* appears in chocolate or cheese varieties. Similarly, *sablés* (shortbread cookies) come in chocolate hazelnut, rosemary Parmesan, or black olive.

Plant yourself in a hot pink banquette and order an "all green" salad of spinach, broccoli, and pistachios, one of five fun monochromatic salad options. The lively *"toute orange"* features carrot, with mild mimolette cheese, grapefruit, and yellow lentils. If you are feeling colorless and *"toute beige,"* order Chinese cabbage, chicken, mushrooms, and pear.

With randomly-hung globe lamps and airy oval skylights, the mood is whimsical, low-key, and friendly. The food is well-prepared, delicious, and unpretentious. Overall, the Delicabar concept really works.

Delicabar's expansive umbrella-shaded outdoor terrace is a pleasant surprise in a department store restaurant.

# Department Store Sweets and Eats

NO CAUSE FOR CONCERN IF A SUGAR CRAVING HITS WHILE SQUEEZING INTO A DESIGNER DRESS IN ONE OF PARIS' SPRAWLING DEPARTMENT STORES—*LES GRANDS MAGASINS* KNOW HOW TO SERVE HUNGRY SHOPPERS WELL WITH A NOTEWORTHY SELECTION OF CAFÉS, RESTAURANTS, AND SWEET COUNTERS. IN FACT, SOME ARE WORTH A VISIT EVEN IF YOU'RE NOT SHOPPING.

Among the highlights is Brasserie Printemps, with its stunning Art Nouveau dome and tranquil atmosphere. Indulge in the tea menu of *profiteroles*, yogurt and pineapple parfaits, or pear rhubarb crumble while admiring the blue and green floral-patterned, stained-glass ceiling. A circular bar centers the room under the dome, with red outer walls and banquettes creating a cozy ambiance. The brasserie lunch menu is perfect for hungrier shoppers.

Printemps' top floor features Déli Cieux, a cafeteria-style, rooftop café with spectacular city views. And of course, the store's Ladurée tea salon and Alain Ducasse *boulangerie* "deli" are always reliable options for satisfying a sweet tooth.

Next door, don't miss Lafayette Gourmet, Galeries Lafayette's all-encompassing array of international gourmet food items. Locals know it as the best bet for finding peanut butter and American pancake mix, but it also offers branches of some of Paris' best *pâtissiers-boulangers*—among them, Dalloyau, Eric Kayser, and Sadaharu Aoki.

Across the street at Galeries Lafayette Maison, Galeries Lafayette's home furnishings store, there's an Amorino *gelateria* and a second-floor café serving some of the city's best hot chocolate and coffee drinks. The pastries are tasty too!

### Printemps Department Store

64, BOULEVARD HAUSSMANN, 9TH ARR.

Telephone 01 42 82 57 87 ✦ Métro HAVRE-CAUMARTIN

Open MONDAY through SATURDAY 9:35AM to 7PM

(THURSDAY until 10PM) ✦ Closed SUNDAY

### Galeries Lafayette

40, BOULEVARD HAUSSMANN, 9TH ARR.

Telephone 01 42 82 34 56 ✦ Métro HAVRE-CAUMARTIN

Open MONDAY through SATURDAY 9:30AM to 7:30PM

(THURSDAY until 9PM) ✦ Closed SUNDAY

# Les Deux Abeilles

189, RUE DE L'UNIVERSITÉ, 7TH ARR.

Telephone + 01 45 55 64 04

Métro + PONT DE L'ALMA

Open MONDAY through SATURDAY 9AM to 7PM + Closed SUNDAY

LADIES WHO LUNCH LOVE LES DEUX ABEILLES. THIS LUNCH / BRUNCH CAFÉ AND TEA SALON DRAWS A CROWD OF WELL-groomed seventh-arrondissement regulars who come for its refined atmosphere and menu of salads, soups, quiches, and of course, desserts.

Start with a gratin of fennel or pumpkin, depending on the season, with a tossed green salad and a glass of red wine. Or savor a salad of roast chicken, steamed vegetables, and toasted pine nuts with a *citron chaud au miel* (hot lemon juice with honey). Waist-watchers enjoy the carrot purée with a warm lentil salad. Others can sink into a *brousse* cheese and broccoli quiche. All are delicious.

For dessert, the raspberry soufflé tart surprises with a walnut meringue over puréed berries. Chocolate lovers can opt for the *fondant chocolat* or a thick brownie, both served with whipped cream. In winter, chestnut cake with a healthy dose of cream is a specialty. Fruit tarts and *clafoutis du jour* are seasonal, while the classic *tarte Tatin* is always available. Lighter options include an apple pear compote *à l'orange* or *fromage blanc* with cream, honey, or jam.

The menu is served all day, making this a nice option for a late afternoon snack of tea and brioche slathered in butter and honey. A highlight of the extensive tea selection is the *infusion Deux Abeilles*, an herbal tea mix of mint, *tilleul*, and *verveine*.

Be sure to reserve for lunch or you'll be relegated to the windowless back smoking section. The front room's floral wallpaper is a bit stodgy but the middle room is bright, with a sky-lit ceiling, black-and-white photos, and a fresh coat of ecru paint.

# Michel Chaudun

149, RUE DE L'UNIVERSITÉ, 7TH ARR.

Telephone + 01 47 53 74 40

Métro + PONT DE L'ALMA

Open MONDAY 10AM to 6PM, TUESDAY through SATURDAY 9:15AM to 6PM

Closed SUNDAY

THE LIFE-SIZE, WHITE CHOCOLATE BUST OF THE PHAROAH TUTANKHAMEN PROMINENTLY DISPLAYED AT THIS SHOP'S entrance is the first clue that Michel Chaudun is no ordinary *chocolatier*. His impressive, true-to-life chocolate creations are well-known around Paris and he is regularly called upon for his special artistic skill. Whether it's a milk chocolate, limited edition, Hermès bag created for the company's anniversary celebration, or bunnies for neighborhood patrons' Easter baskets, Chaudun's mastery is unsurpassed. Baby booties and Eiffel Towers are a few other favorites, popular as gifts.

Chaudun's "plain" chocolate squares are not to be overlooked. Unique flavors include *cerriba* (a peanut and sesame ganache), the *praliné Java*, or the *Sarawak* (an unusual pepper and truffle mix).

Chaudun created his King Tut bust in 1965 for a contest early in his career, years before he opened his eponymous boutique. Today, the bust sits in a sealed glass case as testament to his success. His chocolate creations will keep forever, shop staff says, as long as you keep them at a constant room temperature.

# Rollet Pradier

6, RUE DE BOURGOGNE, 7^TH ARR.

Telephone ✦ 01 45 51 78 36

Métro ✦ INVALIDES or ASSEMBLÉE NATIONALE

Salon de Thé MONDAY through SATURDAY 3PM to 7PM

ROLLET PRADIER, A FIXTURE IN THIS QUIET NEIGHBORHOOD NEAR LES INVALIDES, IS APPRECIATED BY LOCAL BUSINESS people and residents alike for its breads, pastries, and pre-pared foods, as well as its upstairs tea room for an afternoon snack. The classics are all well prepared and reliable. Specialty pastries include *le Bourgogne*, praline and nougat mousse topping a hazelnut and kirsch-soaked sponge cake, or *le Marquis*, bitter chocolate ganache on a hazelnut meringue biscuit. *La Pyramide* features hazelnut mousse and meringue, coated in milk chocolate with nuts. For chocolate-free options, try specialty *blanc manger*, an almond milk custard with seasonal fresh fruit. For breakfast, I like the simple *brioche sucré*, with a tender *crème pâtissière* and sugar-sprinkled center encircled by fresh brioche.

# Secco Pâtisserie-Boulangerie

(FORMERLY BOULANGERIE POUJAURIN)

20, RUE JEAN NICOT, 7ᵀᴴ ARR.

*Telephone* ✦ 01 43 17 35 20

*Métro* ✦ LA TOUR-MAUBOURG

*Open* TUESDAY *through* SATURDAY 8AM *to* 8:30PM

*Closed* SUNDAY *and* MONDAY

WHEN LEGENDARY *BOULANGER* JEAN-LUC POUJAURAN SOLD HIS SHOP IN 2004, PARISIANS WORRIED ABOUT what would happen to this celebrated bastion of excellent French bread. But fans relaxed and pastry lovers cheered when, without touching the revered *boulangerie*, new owner Stephane Secco expanded to make room for his first love—*pâtisseries*.

Sweets no longer take a backseat to breads; an entire new shop next door is now devoted to them. Secco focuses on a limited but excellent line of "flagship pastries" and rotates a seasonal selection, substituting a wild strawberry tart with a *Paris-Brest* as the weather cools, for example. Among the specialties, the lemon and chocolate tarts—called *barquettes* after the crust's oblong, hollow boat-like form—are piled with creamy fillings. The cheesecake (for the many expats and tourists in the neighborhood, Secco says) is made with 0% fat *fromage blanc* (*fromage blanc* comes in either 0%, 20%, or 40% fat), creating a delightfully light version of the traditionally rich Anglo-Saxon dessert. The *millefeuille* is among the most decadent I've seen. It's larger than most, with luscious thick slabs of cream squishing out between pastry layers.

The *madeleines* are among Paris' best. They have an unusual flavor, attributable to a "secret" recipe featuring *sucre vergeoise*, a sticky brown sugar, rather than the refined white variety. Secco also adds a tiny hint of lemon. The cakes' darker color and coarser texture is unique, but wonderful.

Breads remain as excellent as ever, and the *boulangerie* carries delicious sweet breads, too, like *brioche aux chocolat* and sablés with orange zest and raisins.

The original shop, an operating *boulangerie* for more than 100 years, has quaint original décor. And Secco has done an admirable job with the new *pâtisserie*, creating a warm country atmosphere, complete with rough wood beams and a barrel of apples (for sale by the piece, though I can't imagine he sells many!).

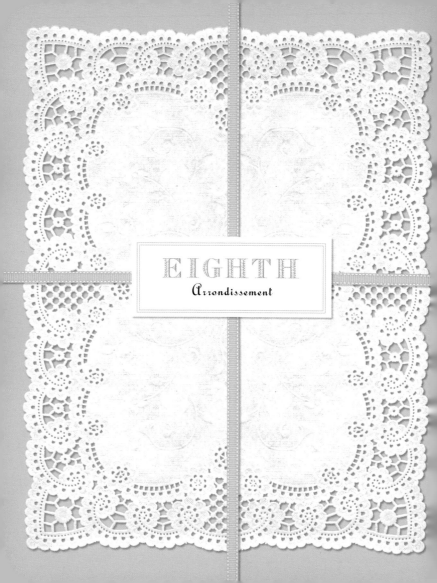

# EIGHTH

*Arrondissement*

# 1728

8, RUE D'ANJOU, 8TH ARR.

Telephone ✦ 01 40 17 04 77

Métro ✦ CONCORDE or MADELEINE

Tea Service MONDAY through SATURDAY 3PM to 6:30PM ✦ Closed SUNDAY

NIBBLING A PASTRY IN 1728'S GLORIOUS EIGHTEENTH-CENTURY INTERIOR IS AMONG PARIS' MOST DECADENT *salon de thé* experiences. Named for the year this stunning Paris home was built, this restaurant's afternoon tea service is a worthwhile splurge.

And, if the setting isn't over-the-top enough, 1728 offers celebrated *pâtissier* Pierre Herme's signature pastries including the *plaisir sucré*, *2000 feuilles*, or the *Ispahan* (See page 159). The tea menu details unique tea blends like the *grand restaurant*, featuring star anise, mint, licorice, coriander, or the *trois étoiles*, described as created by one of the only still-working *herboristes* in Paris.

But atmosphere is the real star of the 1728 show. In its day, the mansion was fashionably located just off Saint Honoré, Paris' newly

chic neighborhood thanks to Louis XV's mistress and eighteenth-century trendsetter, Madame de Pompadour, who was building a house around the corner. Supposedly, she "held court" here while her own home, Hotel d'Evreux (today France's presidential palace), was under construction.

# Le Café Jacquemart-André

JACQUEMART-ANDRÉ MUSEUM

158, BOULEVARD HAUSSMANN, 8TH ARR.

Telephone ◆ 01 42 89 04 91

Métro ◆ MIROMESNIL or SAINT-PHILIPPE-DU-ROULE

Open MONDAY through SATURDAY 11:45AM to 6PM, SUNDAY 11AM to 6PM

Lunch Served DAILY until 3PM

LE CAFÉ JACQUEMART-ANDRÉ, ONE OF PARIS' MOST IMPRESSIVE PASTRY-EATING SETTINGS, IS SET WITHIN A NINETEENTH-century Parisian home, now a museum showcasing residents Edouard André and Nélie Jacquemart's private art collection.

Savor delicious tarts and pastries in the home's original dining room, a spectacular, high-ceilinged space decorated by eighteenth-century decorative artist Giambattista Tiepolo. Original tapestries depict the story of Trojan War hero Achilles. And don't miss the ceiling fresco with monkey's tail that spills over the border, transforming from two- to three-dimensional.

The delicious food is supplied by excellent Paris caterer Stohrer (see page 55). Luncheon salads, named for the collection's artists, include the *Fragonard* (romaine, chicken, and a poached egg, with bacon, Parmesan, and lemon), the *Van Dyck* (foie gras, caramelized figs, smoked duck, and baked apples), or the *Chardin* (mixed greens with chevre, ham, nuts, and tapenade). There is also a quiche or *plat du jour*, served with salad and always delicious.

For dessert, try the super-sweet *gâteau pistache framboises*, chewy pistachio *macaron* wedges sandwiching a rich cream center with fresh raspberries. The double chocolate caramel tart layers dark and white chocolate with a caramelized top. The lemon tart is whipped high with golden, bronzed meringue. Ice cream and *fromage blanc* with berry *coulis* are offered as "lighter" options.

Floor-to-ceiling heavy red velvet drapes muffle sound and give a sense of space and privacy, even in a bustling restaurant, rendering it one of Paris' most enjoyable lunch spots. The terrace in summer, set in the mansion's inner courtyard, is a delight too.

You don't need a museum ticket to enjoy the restaurant. Just skip the ticket line and head on into the café, but if you have time, the collection is one of Paris' artistic gems. The audioguide gives a particularly good history of the collectors and nineteenth-century Paris society.

# Museum Sweet Eats

C AFÉ JACQUEMART ANDRE IS NOT THE ONLY PLACE FOR A DECENT SWEET BITE WHILE ENJOYING ARTISTIC ENLIGHTENMENT.

Musée d'Orsay's stunning restaurant rivals its world-renowned collection in its jaw-dropping Belle Epoque décor. An afternoon tea is available from 3:30-5:30, a perfect spot to rest your legs, indulge in a cake, and bask in the grandeur of the restaurant's *grand salon.* For hungrier museum-goers, lunch is served daily, brunch on Sunday, and dinner on Thursday when the museum stays open late. (Don't confuse this second-floor restaurant with the cramped café on the top level.)

Under the Louvre's arcades, just outside the pyramid, Café Marley's desserts are nothing exceptional, but you can't beat the location for enjoying a drink and taking in the view after a tour of Paris' most famous museum.

The top floor café of the Institut du Monde Arabe has one of Paris' best, and least-known, views. Good (but expensive!) Middle Eastern cuisine, mint tea, and pastries are available.

## Musée D'Orsay

62, RUE DE LILLE, 7TH ARR.

Telephone 01 40 49 48 14 ✦ Métro ASSEMBLÉE NATIONALE

Open TUESDAY through SUNDAY 9:30AM to 6PM

(THURSDAY 9:45PM) ✦ Closed MONDAY

### The Louvre

99, RUE DE RIVOLI, 1ST ARR.

Telephone 01 40 20 51 51 ✦ Métro PALAIS ROYALE-MUSÉE DU LOUVRE

Open WEDNESDAY through TUESDAY 9AM to 6PM (WEDNESDAY
and FRIDAY until 10PM) ✦ Closed TUESDAY

✦

### Institut Du Monde Arabe

1, RUE DES FOSSÉS-SAINT-BERNARD, 5TH ARR.

PLACE MOHAMMED-V

Telephone 01 40 51 38 38 ✦ Métro JUSSIEU or CARDINAL LEMOINE

Open TUESDAY through SUNDAY 10AM to 6PM ✦ Closed MONDAY

# Café Lênotre

PAVILLON ELYSÉE

CARRÉ MARIGNY

10, AVENUE DES CHAMPS ELYSÉES, 8TH ARR.

Télephone ✦ 01 42 65 85 10

Métro ✦ FRANKLIN D. ROOSEVELT

Open DAILY NOON to 10:30PM ✦ Lunch NOON to 2:30 PM

Tea 2:30PM to 7PM, Dinner 7PM to 10:30PM

Closed FOR DINNER on SUNDAY and MONDAY

THE CHAMPS ELYSÉE IS BEST AVOIDED WHEN HUNGRY, AS RIP-OFF TOURIST RESTAURANTS HAVE REPLACED THE GLITZY, glamorous dining establishments of the avenue's storied heyday. However, Café Lênotre is a lifesaving oasis when hunger or sugar cravings strike along this commercial stretch. A restaurant, tearoom, bar/lounge, culinary shop, and cooking school all coexist in the historic, turn-of-the-century Pavillon Elysée along the world's most famous avenue.

The afternoon tea service's lovely *pâtisserie* buffet, appetizingly displayed as you enter the *salon de thé*, is hard to pass up. Priced at 9€ for one *patisserie au choix* or 17€ for as many as you can pile on your plate, it's easy to justify tasting several. The selection is classic and always different, with a recent visit including chocolate éclairs, vanilla *millefeuille*, *macarons*, flans, various fruit tarts, and *feuilles d'automne*, a specialty almond meringue cake with chocolate mousse. The *oeufs à la neige* are striking—white clouds of soft meringue dripping in *crème anglaise*. Miniature *madeleines* and *financiers* are skewered on sticks for easy collecting and adding to your plate. One can also order from the dessert menu—the favorite being the *fondant au chocolat noir*, a molten chocolate cake served with bourbon vanilla ice cream. On the lighter side, try fresh fruit or *fromage blanc*. The "famous Lênotre hot chocolate" gets top billing on the menu, made with "intense dark chocolate" and pure cream. If that's too over-the-top, one of Lênotre's exotic teas rounds out the perfect afternoon snack.

Salty snacks like pumpkin soup, quiche lorraine or chicken or smoked salmon sandwiches are available all day. During meal times, a full menu is served.

The dining room's floor-to-ceiling atrium windows create a bright space, accentuated by orange banquettes and views of the leafy square outside. The "lounge" smoking section is a decidedly hipper atmosphere, with sunken leather chairs, low tables, and a sleek bar. High molded, frescoed ceilings juxtapose against a painted orange wall covered with carefully displayed Lênotre products for sale.

Lênotre's Pavillon Elysée, is essentially a temple to Lênotre, France's original *pâtissier* and caterer, opened by Gaston Lênotre in 1957. It expanded into a *traiteur*, or prepared food boutique, and quickly became Paris' most chic caterer. Today, Lênotre has sixteen boutiques around Paris, three restaurants (including Pavillon Elysée) and several other outlets in France. Best known for catering, Lênotre's roots are firmly planted in *pâtisseries*.

# Dalloyau

101, RUE DU FAUBOURG-SAINT-HONORÉ, 8TH ARR.

*Telephone* ✦ 01 42 99 90 00

*Métro* ✦ SAINT-PHILIPPE-DU-ROULE

*Open* DAILY 8AM to 9PM

ALLOYAU IS ONE OF FRANCE'S BEST-KNOWN AND OLDEST *MAISONS DE GASTRONOMIE*, A PERENNIAL BOUTIQUE OFFERing prepared foods, catering, breads, and desserts.

But for pastry lovers, more important is its illustrious claim to the creation of *l'Opéra*. This now-ubiquitous *gâteau par excellence* featuring alternating layers of coffee-soaked almond cake, coffee cream, and chocolate, is an adored *pâtisserie* staple. To fête the *Opéra*'s fiftieth birthday in 2006, Dalloyau launched the *Opéra rock*, "updating" with almond and caramel creams, and a chocolate raspberry ganache interior. It's attractive and tasty, but hasn't supplanted the classic version's rank as Parisians' favorite *entremet*.

Dalloyau does the classics well, and regularly launches innovative flavors, like the *neige d'été*, liqueur-soaked almond cake with vanilla cream, fresh pineapple, and mango, and caramelized *feuilleté* flakes. The *exquise convoitise* is a striking chocolate and purple berry striped layer cake. A recently featured "*macaron* of the month" was vibrant red cherry cream.

Most Dalloyau shops have pleasant *salons de thé*, excellent stops for resting weary legs, sipping a freshly squeezed *jus d'orange*, or nibbling a salty or sweet snack.

# Additional Locations

5, BOULEVARD BEAUMARCHAIS, 4TH ARR.
Telephone 01 48 87 89 88 ◆ Métro BASTILLE
Open EVERY DAY 9AM to 9PM

2, PLACE EDMOND ROSTAND, 6TH ARR.
Telephone 01 43 29 31 10 ◆ Métro LUXEMBOURG
Open EVERY DAY 9AM to 8:30PM

63, RUE DE GRENELLE, 7TH ARR.
Telephone 01 45 49 95 30 ◆ Métro RUE DU BAC or SEVRES-BABYLONE
Open EVERY DAY 9AM to 8:30PM

69, RUE DE LA CONVENTION, 15TH ARR.
Telephone 01 45 77 84 27 ◆ Métro BOUCICAULT
Open SUNDAY through THURSDAY 9AM-8PM
FRIDAY and SATURDAY 9AM to 7:30PM

## Lafayette Gourmet

48–52, BOULEVARD HAUSSMANN, 9TH ARR.
Telephone 01 53 20 05 00 ◆ Métro HAVRE-CAUMARTIN
or CHAUSSÉE D'ANTIN-LA FAYETTE
Open MONDAY through SATURDAY 9:30AM to 8:30PM (THURSDAY 9PM)

# Fauchon

24–26–30, PLACE DE LA MADELEINE, 8TH ARR.

Telephone ✦ 01 70 39 38 00

Métro ✦ MADELEINE

Pâtisserie and Traiteur MONDAY through SATURDAY 8AM to 9PM

Boulangerie 8AM to 8PM ✦ Boutique 9AM to 8PM

OPENED IN 1886, FAUCHON IS A *GRAND CLASSIQUE* AT THIS BUSY PLACE DE LA MADELEINE JUNCTION OF FRANCE'S premiere *gastronome* boutiques. Chocolates, candies, jams, pastries, coffees, and catered/prepared foods—Fauchon does everything well.

Among its excellent *pâtisseries*, Fauchon is known for its creative spirit, balancing its repertoire of classics with a constantly evolving collection of *nouveautés*. These whimsical creations are often an updated play on a traditional favorite or a "limited edition" to celebrate a holiday. Among the house specialty éclairs, for example, dark brown chocolate and *café* specimens coexist with purple fig or black-and-white-striped "tuxedo" varieties. White éclairs with green spots contain a surprise white chocolate and green tea filling. Bright yellow mango varieties herald the arrival of spring. *Chez* Fauchon, each season sees the release of new flavors and signature cakes. Still, the classics persist in their popularity—the *millefeuille*, *baba au rhum*, or lemon tarts. The *megève* is a Fauchon favorite, *gianduja* chocolate mousse sandwiched by vanilla and chocolate meringues.

At Christmastime, don't miss Fauchon boutique's *marrons glacés*, rated "best in France" by French guide *Gault Millau*. Using only chestnuts from Turin, Italy ("the best," according to Fauchon's candy buyer Damien Colieu), the special house recipe calls to soak them in syrup for seven to eight days to achieve the perfect sugary coating.

Catty-corner to the boutique, the newly revamped *boulangerie* showcases the company's inventive flair, featuring a *"bar à madeleines"* where you can choose from 14 flavors of the little cake. Sweet varieties include hazelnut pistachio, honey, caramel, saffron, or chestnut—super sweet with a dollop of chestnut inside—while salty choices include black pepper, truffle, seaweed, or my favorite, sesame (sugary and salty at the same time with a nut-flavored, soft interior).

Brioches also come in a multitude of choices—notably with chocolate, raspberry, lemon, or gingerbread filling. The *boulangerie* offers breads, *viennoiserie*, and light lunch items with a few tables for *"snacking sur place."* Fresh fruit juices and coffee drinks are also available.

# Dream Job:

## An Interview with Fauchon's Candy Buyer

---

AMIEN COLIEU ALWAYS LOVED TO EAT. WHEN HE SOUGHT A CAREER THAT WOULD COMBINE HIS LOVE OF FOOD WITH HIS INTEREST IN BIOLOGY, HE ENDED UP WITH WHAT MANY WOULD CONSIDER A DREAM JOB—THE CHOCOLATE BUYER FOR FAUCHON, ONE OF FRANCE'S OLDEST AND MOST REVERED *BOUTIQUES DE GASTRONOMIE*. TODAY, THE TWENTY-NINE YEAR OLD OVERSEES PRODUCT DEVELOPMENT AND SALES FOR THE COMPANY'S *CONFISERIE* (CANDY), *CONFITURE* (JAMS), AND *BISCUITS* (COOKIES AND CAKES), AND HIS TRUE PASSION—CHOCOLATE.

His job is not to be taken lightly since Fauchon sells seventy tons of chocolate a year. More importantly, he says, the Fauchon name is an international symbol of France. Chocolate serves as an ambassador, and it is his job to ensure the quality of the brand. Any chocolate stamped with the Fauchon *marque* is an instant bestseller—a symbol of prestige and a favorite among tourists buying gifts to take home, Colieu says. Inside those branded gift boxes, best-selling flavors include the praline and the *carre d'or* (*gianduja* chocolate with a whole hazelnut), a worldwide best-seller that is especially popular in the Middle East.

Tourist sales are important, but the French consume a lot of Fauchon sweets too. Half of Fauchon's chocolate is sold during the Christmas season, mirroring country-wide buying habits. (By contrast, in the Japanese market, 90% of chocolate is bought for Valentine's Day—almost all of it by women.)

Jams—also popular gift products—are more consistent sellers throughout the year. Fauchon sells 350 tons of jam annually, 60% of it in Japan. The classics like apricot and strawberry are top sellers, but special flavors like rose petal are popular too. Americans love any red fruit variety, he says.

As an *agroalimentary* engineer by training, Colieu studied the science of transforming raw materials into finished food products, including production techniques, hygiene, and security. He then got a master's degree in marketing, and for the Fauchon position pursued several chocolate-making courses and apprenticeships.

When Colieu arrived at Fauchon three years ago, his challenge was to increase quality, which meant replacing suppliers that weren't up to snuff. Today, all Fauchon chocolate is supplied by one hand-picked French producer. Each product line has just one producer to ensure consistency and quality, he says.

So how does Colieu describe a good chocolate? First, it's a chocolate that you enjoy the experience of eating—the smell, the taste, the texture, he says. A ganache should be well balanced—the chocolate must not overpower the ganache, and vice versa. The outer chocolate shell should crack gently, allowing your teeth to sink inside. There should be a strong cocoa flavor, not too much taste of cream, not too acidic. Finally, chocolates should be made only with cocoa butter, not vegetable fats, he adds. Colieu's personal favorite is milk chocolate, not too sweet and with a distinct milky taste.

# Galler

114, BOULEVARD HAUSSMANN, 8TH ARR.

Telephone ◆ 01 45 22 33 49

Métro ◆ MIROMESNIL

Open MONDAY through SATURDAY 10AM to 7PM

AMONG *CHOCOLATIERS* PUSHING THE LIMITS OF CREATIVITY, BELGIAN JEAN GALLER IS AT THE TOP OF THE LIST. TEAMING up with florist Daniel Ost, the duo macerates chocolate in crushed flower petals, delicately infusing it with rose, violet, jasmin, or orange flower *parfums*. Amazingly, they are delicious. His latest Japanese-inspired line, *kaori* (meaning fragrance or perfume), is an unconventional system of chocolate-flavored sticks that you dip in one of three pots—green tea and poppyseed, *yuzu* (a Japanese citrus fruit), or cocoa and orange zest. The sticks (or *batons*) come in six varieties—saffron, cardamom, ginger, strawberry balsamic, among others—enabling the creation of forty-two possible flavor combinations. Traditionalists appreciate Galler's pure chocolate bars, truffles, and fruit candied jellies.

### ◆ ◆ ◆ Additional Location ◆ ◆ ◆

13, RUE D'ALIGRE, 12TH ARR.

Telephone 01 43 40 34 45 ◆ Métro LEDRU-ROLLIN

Open TUESDAY through FRIDAY 9AM to 1:30PM and 3PM to 8PM

SATURDAY 9AM to 8PM ◆ Closed MONDAY EXCEPT the THREE

MONDAYS before CHRISTMAS

# Hédiard

21 PLACE DE LA MADELEINE, 8TH ARR.

Telephone ✦ 01 43 12 88 99

Métro ✦ MADELEINE

Boutique Open MONDAY through SATURDAY 9AM to 9PM ✦ Closed SUNDAY

Tea Service Open MONDAY through SATURDAY, 3PM to 6PM

SUGAR LOVERS SHOULD NOT PASS HÉDIARD WITHOUT STOP-PING TO ADMIRE (EVEN BETTER, TO TASTE) HÉDIARD'S *PÂTES des fruits*. Proudly showcased front and center just inside the shop's entrance, you can't miss the colorful stacks of fruit "jellies" that are this *traiteur*'s specialty. The vivid multi-hued squares are impressive by their extensive selection alone—grapefruit, fig, apricot, Reine Claude, passion fruit, kiwi, blackberry, peach, mandarin, even guava, green apple, date and lime ginger, to name a few of the twenty-six different varieties—almost any fruit imaginable! A special house recipe distills the freshest, highest quality fruit's essence, creating the intense experience of biting into what seems like the ripest, most perfectly sweet fruit.

Hédiard has provided Parisians with exotic and novelty foods since 1854. Indeed, the boutique is a gourmet's delight, stocked with unusual spices, jams, fruit cakes, gingerbread, almond cookies, candied chestnuts, fruit-soaked liqueurs, and regional specialties like rose biscuits from Reims and *crepes dentelle* cookies from Brittany. Today, Hédiard also has a thriving take-out business, with savory and sweet delicacies available for sale at the shop's counter.

The *service du thé* in the restaurant upstairs is a good place to sample

Hédiard's pastries, offering a pot of tea and a *patisserie au choix* from the dessert case for 12€. Hediard's pastry specialty—the *mille-feuille*—is "free form" take on the classic, with dollops of vanilla cream on lightly layered flaky pastry sheets. The pastry almost has a salty tang, rendering it less overwhelmingly sweet than most varieties. The *Hédiard prestige* is an original house creation—a vanilla mousse with a tropical fruit cream interior. La Table de Hédiard's atmosphere is nothing to write home about, but the tea service is a nice place to indulge after whetting your appetite in the shop downstairs.

## ✦ ✦ ✦ Additional Locations ✦ ✦ ✦

31 AVENUE GEORGE V, 8TH ARR.
Telephone 01 47 20 44 44 ✦ Métro GEORGES V
Open MONDAY through FRIDAY 9AM to 9PM
SATURDAY and SUNDAY 9AM to 8PM

106 BOULEVARD DE COURCELLES, 17TH ARR.
Telephone 01 47 63 32 14 ✦ Métro COURCELLES
Open MONDAY through SATURDAY 9:30AM to 10PM ✦ Closed SUNDAY

70 AVENUE PAUL DOUMER, 16TH ARR.
Telephone 01 45 04 51 92 ✦ Métro LA MUETTE
Open MONDAY through SATURDAY 9AM to 10PM ✦ Closed SUNDAY

GALERIE DES FRESQUES, 12TH ARRONDISEMENT
Telephone 01 46 28 04 15 ✦ Métro GARE DE LYON
Open DAILY 8:30AM to 8:30PM

# Ladurée

16, RUE ROYALE, 8TH ARR.

Telephone ◆ 01 42 60 21 79

Métro ◆ CONCORDE or MADELEINE

Open MONDAY through SATURDAY 8:30AM to 7PM, SUNDAY 10AM to 7PM

FOR MANY, LADURÉE IS *THE* QUINTESSENTIAL FRENCH *PÂTISSERIE*. DIRECTOR SOFIA COPPOLA TURNED TO ITS eye-popping pastries to illustrate the decadence of the eighteenth-century French royal court in her film *Marie Antoinette*. Ladurée's over-the-top, dripping custard cakes and glamorous *petits fours* depict perfectly the excess of Versailles life (even if anachronistic since Ladurée wasn't founded until 1862).

And with good reason. Almost too pretty to eat, Ladurée's creations look so perfect that you want to wallow in their splendor. But don't skip tasting them. Start with a specialty like the *Saint-Honoré rose-framboise*, a whipped puff of raspberry compote, rose flower cream, and fresh raspberries, delicately balanced on a buttery *sablé* crust. Then move on to *le baiser Ladurée* (Ladurée's Kiss), layered almond

cake, fresh strawberries and cream, with a light touch of poppy flower. Try a pistachio, *fleur d'orange*, or rose *religieuse*, a vibrant take on a staid brown-frosted classic whose name means "nun," which the squat pastry is meant to resemble.

Ladurée is perhaps best-known for its *macarons*, which it claims to have created.

Competition is stiff for this currently trendy sandwich cookie, with *pâtissiers* trying to outdo one another with innovative, and sometimes wacky, flavors. Crunching slightly at impact, then turning chewy and revealing intensely-flavored cream inside, Ladurée's vivid-hued *macarons* hold their own. Ladurée sets each almond flour cookie aside for two days after baking to achieve the perfect texture and consistency before it joins the colorful assortment for sale at the pastry counter. As a tribute to its most famous progeny, every season Ladurée adds a new flavor to its roster of staples (chocolate, vanilla, coffee, hazelnut praline, rose, pistachio, raspberry, and lemon). Seasonal flavors include spring's violet, summer's coconut and lime basil, and winter's chestnut and licorice.

Ladurée's artistic shop window displays, showcasing bright piled-high *macaron* cakes, stop passersby in their tracks. Also renowned is the *salon de thé*, which has an illustrious history as one of Paris' most popular *fin-de-siècle* meeting places. It was among Paris' first tearooms and an immediate success as a socially acceptable place for women to congregate without a male escort, as was the custom in Paris cafés at the time. Ladurée retains its charm as an alluring spot for a pastry and tea (or lunch and a coffee). Still in its original rue Royale shop, much of the décor remains, including a ceiling fresco by Jules Cheret, a famous designer of the period.

Ladurée's beautifully packaged chocolates are so lovely that it is my preferred chocolatier for gifts. I also never miss an opportunity to visit the rue Bonaparte candy shop (next door to the pâtisserie) for its nineteenth-century décor (actually built in the 1990s, but with all original nineteenth-century furnishings). So exquisite that it doesn't matter that it hasn't been there forever, it is a treat just to peak at the ceiling fresco of puffy, pale blue clouds hanging over the delicate glass chandelier. The signature light-green boxes line one mirrored wall, while nineteenth-century chocolate molds adorn the other. The third wall houses streams of different colored ribbon for tying up the packaged goodies. Don't miss the chocolate fresco tiled floor—my favorite.

### ✦ ✦ ✦ Additional Locations ✦ ✦ ✦

21, RUE BONAPARTE, 6TH ARR.

Telephone 01 44 07 64 87 ✦ Métro SAINT-GERMAIN-DES-PRÉS

Open MONDAY through SATURDAY 8:30AM to 7:30PM

SUNDAY and HOLIDAYS 10AM to 7:30PM

✦

75, AVENUE DES CHAMPS-ELYSÉES, 8TH ARR.

Telephone 01 40 75 08 75 ✦ Métro GEORGE V

Open DAILY 7:30AM to 11:30PM ✦ Restaurant 7:30AM to 12:30AM

✦

62, BOULEVARD HAUSSMANN, 9TH ARR.

IN THE PRINTEMPS DEPARTMENT STORE

Telephone 01 42 82 40 10 ✦ Métro HAVRE-CAUMARTIN

Open MONDAY through SATURDAY 9:35AM to 7PM (THURSDAY 10PM)

Closed SUNDAY

# Minamoto Kitchoan Paris

17 PLACE DE LA MADELEINE, 8TH ARR.

Telephone ✦ 01 40 06 91 28

Métro ✦ MADELEINE

Boutique Open MONDAY through SATURDAY, 10AM to 7PM ✦ Closed SUNDAY

Salon de Thé 11:30AM to 6:30PM

EVEN A DEVOTED FRENCH PASTRY BUFF LIKE ME CAN OCCA-
SIONALLY USE A BREAK FROM THE MOUNDS OF CREAM AND
chocolate piled on buttery cakes and tarts. That's when I get
on my bike, pedal over to Madeleine and retreat to Minamoto Kitcho-
an's Japanese *pâtisserie*. There, I get my fix of azuki bean, sesame and
green tea sweets in a tranquil corner of this Japanese tearoom.

After a nourishing bowl of udon noodle soup, I'll tuck into an
*anmitsu*, the centuries-old Japanese favorite dessert that embodies
the union of traditional Japanese and occidental pastry-making arts.
Transparent cubes of agar-agar (a seaweed) float with glutinous balls
of sticky rice, cherries and apricots, and a sweet compote of red azuki
beans. Sugar cane juice is served on the side, and vanilla, green tea or
sesame ice cream is optional, but indispensable. Don't miss the black
sesame, which lends a nutty flavor that makes the dish!

Another specialty is the impressive *coupe glacé crousti-moelleuse à l'Azuki*, a Japanese version of an ice cream sundae. Scoops of red bean ice cream are served in a huge bowl with sweetened red beans, sponge cake pieces, red bean compote and tons of whipped cream. The mâcha version replaces the red bean with green tea.

It pays to be adventurous when ordering, as the written descriptions are hard for an occidental palate to imagine and don't do the sweets justice.

Stop in the front shop on your way out and pick up some wrapped pastries to go, like the *génoise au thé vert*, a delicate, almost fruity cake stuffed with white azuki bean cream and green tea, or the *tendre lait*, a kidney bean cream sandwich cookie.

# La Petite Rose

11, BOULEVARD DE COURCELLES, 8TH ARR.

*Telephone* ✦ 01 45 22 07 27

*Métro* ✦ VILLIERS

*Open* THURSDAY *through* TUESDAY 10AM *to* 7:30PM ✦ *Closed* WEDNESDAY

LA PETITE ROSE SPECIALIZES IN CHOCOLATE—PASTRIES, CAKES, BROWNIES, HOT CHOCOLATE, AND CANDIES—ALL HOME-made and ready for sampling in this unpretentious *pâtisserie/* tea salon. At first glance, the sweet selection is spare, and the pink room uninteresting. But upon closer examination (and tasting), you'll discover mouthwatering creative, chocolate marvels like the *Alexandria*, a chocolate biscuit topped with praline *feuilleté*, hazelnut cream, and chocolate mousse, or the *Valentin*, raspberry *crème brulée* with fresh berries dolloped over chocolate mousse and crust. If you are not into all the fancy flavors, go for the straight-up, deceptively simple *tout chocolat*. Non-chocolate fans, try the *ange*, a light cheese mousse with raspberry *coulis* or a selection of *macarons* with tea.

A light lunch menu of soups, salads, and vegetable or ham and endive tarts is served from noon until 3 p.m. Although La Petite Rose is not set up with a traditional pastry counter, locals who spot tempting treats in the window stop in and have them prettily wrapped to go.

# NINTH

## Arrondissement

# A La Mère de Famille

35, RUE DU FAUBOURG MONTMARTRE, 9TH ARR.

*Telephone* ✦ 01 47 70 83 69

*Métro* ✦ LE PELETIER

*Open* MONDAY *through* SATURDAY 9:30AM *to* 8PM, SUNDAY 10AM *to* 1PM

WHEN A LA MÈRE DE FAMILLE OPENED ITS DOORS IN 1761 IN THIS CORNER STOREFRONT ON RUE DU FAUBOURG Montmartre, candy's popularity in the Versailles courts had already caught on with the rest of Parisians, making it a favorite eighteenth-century indulgence for those who could afford it.

Not only has A La Mère de Famille remained in its original location, but its candies have stayed true to its roots. Specialties today still include past favorites like *pâtes des fruits* (candied fruit jellies), *pâtes d'amandes* (almond paste or marzipan molded into fruits and animals), and *calissons*, an almond and candied fruit specialty from Aix-en-Provence, created in 1493 for a royal wedding feast. Today, A La Mère de Famille offers six *calisson* vari-eties in addition to traditional melon— pistachio, nut, coffee, armagnac, lemon, and orange. Almond paste candies were very popular in the shop's early days, while mint and caramel candies like *Le Negus*, still sold here, were all the rage in the nineteenth century. Today, choco-late is the shop's best-selling confection, with specialties ranging from solid dark

tablets to truffles to liqueur-filled varieties.

In a nod to tradition, the shop also still carries nuts, raisins, dried fruits, homemade jams, and packages of old-fashioned cookies, biscuits, and gingerbreads. There is a small shelf in the back with "modern" candies, but otherwise, not much has changed. The shop's colorful, traditional packages make cute gifts.

## ✦ ✦ ✦ Additional Locations ✦ ✦ ✦

107, RUE JOUFFROY D'ABBANS, 17TH ARR.
Telephone 01 47 63 15 15 ✦ Métro WAGRAM
Open MONDAY through SATURDAY 10AM to 7:30PM ✦ Closed SUNDAY

30, RUE LEGENDRE, 17TH ARR.
Telephone 01 47 63 52 94 ✦ Métro MALESHERBES
Open TUESDAY through SATURDAY 10AM to 8PM, SUNDAY 10AM to 1PM
MONDAY 1PM to 7PM

47, RUE CLER, 7TH ARR.
Telephone 01 45 55 29 74 ✦ Métro ECOLE MILITAIRE
Open TUESDAY through SATURDAY 9:30AM to 7:30PM
SUNDAY 10AM to 1PM, MONDAY 1PM to 7:30PM

39, RUE DU CHERCHE MIDI, 6TH ARR.
Telephone 01 42 22 49 99 ✦ Métro SAINT-SULPICE
Open TUESDAY through SATURDAY 10AM to 7:30PM
MONDAY 1PM to 7:30PM ✦ Closed SUNDAY

# Arnaud Delmontel

39, RUE DES MARTYRS, 9TH ARR.

Telephone ✦ 01 48 78 29 33

Métro ✦ NOTRE-DAME-DE-LORETTE

Open WEDNESDAY through MONDAY 7AM to 8:30PM ✦ Closed TUESDAY

DELMONTEL IS BEST-KNOWN FOR HIS TRADEMARK *CHOCO' MISS* KID'S TREAT, A RASPBERRY CREAM AND CHOCOLATE ganache-filled biscuit in the stylized form of a Japanese cartoon character. But for grownups, this *pâtisserie-boulangerie*'s highlight is its rotating selection of original *cakes maison*: four-spice ginger, cardamom date, lemon poppyseed, raisin fig mint or apricot basil. Sablés are another good choice, particularly the *croustinoix* or the *Alsacien*, with a crunchy baked nut exterior and interior layers of fruit jam. *Financiers* come in fascinating flavors like fig lavender. Delmontel's specialty pastries include the *mara des bois*, strawberry mousse and fennel cream on a biscuit crust, or the *adagio*, filled with pistachio and chocolate cream. The shop has an excellent selection of prepared salads and savory take-out options.

### ✦ ✦ ✦ Additional Location ✦ ✦ ✦

57, RUE DAMRÉMONT, 18TH ARR.

Métro ✦ LAMARCK-CAULAINCOURT

Open TUESDAY through SATURDAY 7AM to 8:30PM

SUNDAY 7AM to 2:30PM ✦ Closed MONDAY

# Aurore Capucine

3, RUE DE ROCHECHOUART, 9TH ARR.

*Telephone* ✦ 01 48 78 16 20

*Metro* ✦ CADET

*Open* TUESDAY *through* FRIDAY 11AM *to* 8PM SATURDAY 11AM *to* 7:30PM ✦

*Closed* SUNDAY *and* MONDAY.

AURORE CAPUCINE'S OWNER MADAME PETIT LIKES TO DO THINGS A LITTLE BIT DIFFERENTLY. PETIT EXPLAINS THAT SHE AND her husband aren't interested in offering the same pastries as every other Paris *pâtisserie*. Petit has run the shop with her *pâtissier* husband for nineteen years.

The Petits' taste for the uncommon is clear in specialties that feature flavors like *piment d'Espelette* (a chili from the Basque region), *fleur de sel*, and *eau de geranium* (geranium water). Their favored ingredients—flower essences and herbs—shine in their *sablés*, the shop's best-known house recipe. Crunchy and not-too-sweet, neighborhood fans appreciate the unusual varieties of violet, rose, basil parsley, *herbes de Provence*, or cinnamon, to name a few.

The Petits enjoy experimenting with foreign-influenced desserts like *le Nuremberg*, an Austrian

five-spice bread, or *le délice*, an Eastern European ginger and acacia honey treat. Most start with a French base and add an international twist. The shop's famous buns are pure butter brioche worked into a round bun shape, rather than baked in a brioche mold, and filled with chocolate bits or golden raisins. Baking the dough in a free-form shape is enough to alter the taste of the brioche, according to Madame Petit.

Offerings are seasonal, with winter choices heavy on citrus fruits, chestnut, and chocolate, while spring and summer options bring lighter, fruitier pastries. From October through April (chocolate season), Parisians come from all over to stuff their Christmas tables and Easter baskets with Aurore Capucine's famous, homemade chocolates.

# Fouquet

36, RUE LAFFITTE, 9TH ARR.

Telephone + 01 47 70 85 00

Métro + NOTRE-DAME-DE-LORETTE or LE PELETIER

Open MONDAY through FRIDAY 10AM to 6:30PM

I LOVE FOUQUET BECAUSE, UNLIKE MOST *CHOCOLATIERS*, THEY GIVE OUT SAMPLES. EAGER SHOP STAFF ASK YOUR PREFERENCES, make suggestions, and offer tastes before purchase. And of course, the chocolates always meet (and usually exceed) proud Fouquet staffers' glowing reviews.

Specialties include *les pralinés*, as well as chocolate, caramel, and fruit ganaches. Caramel lovers shouldn't miss the *Salvador*, a house recipe of soft chewy caramel with a hard caramel coating.

Fouquet has been a family-run business since it opened at this original location in 1852.

### + + + Additional Location + + +

22, RUE FRANÇOIS 1ER, 8TH ARR.

Telephone 01 47 23 30 36 + Métro FRANKLIN D. ROOSEVELT

Open MONDAY through SATURDAY 10AM to 7:30PM

# TENTH
## Arrondissement

# Du Pain et des Idées

34, RUE YVES TOUDIC, 10TH ARR.

*Telephone* ✦ 01 42 40 44 52

*Métro* ✦ RÉPUBLIQUE or JACQUES BONSERGENT

*Open* MONDAY *through* FRIDAY 7:30AM *to* 2:30PM *and* 3:30PM *to* 8PM

*Closed* SATURDAY *and* SUNDAY

TO MAKE BREAD, ACCORDING TO *BOULANGER* CHRISTOPHE VASSEUR, IS *"NOURRIR L'ÂME"*—TO NOURISH THE SOUL. It's simple, but fundamental, says Vasseur, who at age thirty-three traded a business world job for the life of a *boulanger*. He says that his new profession is "even more beautiful than I'd imagined. I am creating a product, something people appreciate."

It's easy to appreciate anything he makes, but his breads and *viennoiserie* are best. Vasseur's specialty is his divine *chausson à la pomme fraîche*, a flaky turnover filled with fresh cooked apple, sometimes made with seasonal fruits such as figs. The *san cristan*, a pastry twist wrapped with pistachio cream, is one of the most delicious I've ever tasted. A neighborhood favorite, *brioche la mouna* is a special Provençal recipe that you won't find elsewhere in Paris, buttery and dense with a hint of *fleur d'orange*. Vasseur's staff will slice you a slab from a long loaf according to your preference: the crusty end or the soft center, *"bien cuit"* (well-cooked, with a golden crust) or *"moins cuit"* (chewy and undercooked, how I love it), with a top-crust and with or without sugar crystals. As a devotee of the fluffy white baguette, healthier whole grain options never interested me until I discovered Vasseur's *boule aux céréales*. Deep brown-crusted, dense with crunchy

seeds, it's hands-down the best of its kind.

Once Vasseur decided to follow his dream, he applied his business savvy to his shop, carefully scouting out the neighborhood until he found—and exquisitely renovated—an existing *boulangerie* dating from 1889. Then he set to work getting up at 3:30 a.m. to make bread and *viennoiserie*. His recipe: Serve the highest-quality, classic favorites while catering to his neighborhood clientele's contemporary tastes. It seems surprising that this approach would be unusual in a country where anything *artisanal* is revered, but it is hard to find this level of quality, and Vasseur's success is testament to that. Vasseur's baked goods are expensive, his shop gets little random walk-in trade, and it's surrounded by other *boulangeries*. This is proof, he says, that he makes an exceptional product.

Those in the know flock to Du Pain et des Ideés after 4:30 p.m. Monday through Thursday, and after 11 a.m. on Fridays to buy up *pain des amis* as it comes out of the oven. Usually sold out before it has a chance to cool down, this unique recipe created by Vasseur is similar to foccacia only with a thicker crust and chewier inside.

### ✦ ✦ ✦ Additional Location ✦ ✦ ✦

24, RUE SAINT-MARTIN, 4TH ARR.

Telephone 01 48 87 46 17 ✦ Métro CHÂTELET

Open MONDAY through FRIDAY 7:30AM to 8PM

# ELEVENTH
## Arrondissement

# Demoulin Chocolatier

6, BOULEVARD VOLTAIRE, 11ᵀᴴ ARR.

Telephone ✦ 01 47 00 58 20

Métro ✦ RÉPUBLIQUE

Open TUESDAY through SUNDAY 8:30AM to 7:30PM ✦ Closed MONDAY

ANY *BOULANGER* OR *PÂTISSIER* WILL TELL YOU IT'S IMPOSSIBLE TO MAKE BOTH BREAD AND PASTRIES, OR AT LEAST make them both well. This is confusing since most shops are expected to offer both, and thus are labeled "*Pâtissier-Boulanger*," making it difficult to identify the *real pâtisseries*.

Demoulin is a rare *pâtisserie* that is only a *pâtisserie*, selling just pastries and chocolates. The cakes are displayed in the window with carefully marked descriptions, with the most prominent placement given to the *délice*, the specialty of the house. A caramelized crust coats layers of vanilla cream, chocolate whipped cream, and almond sponge cake. My favorite, the *zazou*, is unique to Demoulin. A chocolate-coated meringue filled with caramel cream, I'm amazed this pastry hasn't been copied and offered elsewhere in Paris. The *soufflé framboise* is delicious, a *sablé* tart crust with raspberries topped by beautiful *crème Chiboust* (pastry cream lightened with whipped egg whites) and lightly browned in the oven.

Demoulin also specializes in chocolates, with classics like hazelnut or raspberry ganache as well as more creative inventions like ginger-filled ganache or ganache infused with lemongrass or Earl Grey tea.

# How to Become a Pâtissier

IN FRANCE, THE PATH TO BECOME A *PÂTISSIER* IS STRUCTURED AND DEMANDING. AT THE MOST BASIC LEVEL, ONE MUST COMPLETE A TWO-YEAR C.A.P. (*CERTIFICAT D'APTITUDE PROFESSIONNELLE*) DEGREE, AN EXTENSIVE CURRICULUM THAT ENCOMPASSES *PÂTISSERIE, BOULANGERIE, CONFISERIE, CHOCOLATERIE*. AFTER THE INITIAL STAGE, ONE CAN CHOOSE A SPECIALIZED ROUTE OF EITHER *BOULANGERIE* OR *PÂTISSERIE*, WITH THE *PÂTISSERIE* SPECIALIZATION COVERING CANDY, CHOCOLATE, AND ICE CREAM MASTERY IN ADDITION TO PASTRIES.

A SAMPLING OF COURSES MIGHT INCLUDE:

+ Techniques and Preparation of Basic *Pâtisserie*
+ Conservation Techniques
+ Working with Chocolate
+ Ice Cream Preparation
+ Quality Control
+ *Pâtisserie* Personnel
+ Design and Decoration Techniques
+ Microbiology
+ Alimentary Parasitology

Notoriously difficult, the basic C.A.P. curriculum also requires mastery of subjects like math, chemistry, physics, and geography. After passing the degree, aspiring *pâtissiers* become apprentices in a *pâtisserie*, usually two grueling years of hard work and early hours.

Most *pâtissiers*-to-be start their studies at high school age. It's good to start young because you need lots of energy, says Stephane Varin of Julien (see page 23), who decided to become a *pâtissier* at age fourteen, started his degree at fifteen-and-a-half, and began working at eighteen.

By contrast, it is becoming increasingly acceptable to make a mid-career shift into the field, like Christophe Vasseur of Du Pain et Des Idees who went back to school at age thirty to pursue his dream of being a *boulanger*. The field is also becoming more accessible to women—who traditionally have minded the front of the shop—although they are still underrepresented in the kitchen.

# La Pharmacie

22, RUE JEAN-PIERRE-TIMBAUD, 11TH ARR.

Telephone ✦ 01 43 38 04 99

Métro ✦ OBERKAMPF

Open TUESDAY and WEDNESDAY 11AM to 6PM

THURSDAY through SUNDAY 11AM to 11PM ✦ Closed MONDAY

ORGANIC OPTIONS ARE LIMITED IN PARIS, BUT ON THE RISE. IN THE UNDERSTATED-HIP OBERKAMPF AREA, LA PHARMACIE opened in 2005 offering a 100% organic (*biologique*) menu, desserts included.

The desserts are classics with a twist. The pear tart has a touch of coffee in the *crème pâtissière*, quite a surprise when you are expecting the usual pear tart. The *fondant chocolat* tastes a bit more traditional. The lunch menu changes daily, generally offering a soup, a quiche, or a vegetarian couscous. More than fifty types of teas are sorted by color and variety—green, black, oolong, white, aromatic green, aromatic black, blends, herbal, and so on.

As the name suggests, La Pharmacie's corner-store space spent many years as a pharmacy, and the owners kept its original façade and walls of antique glass cabinets. The atmosphere is mellow, with classical music, newspapers strewn about, and a young, chic clientele.

# TWELFTH
## Arrondissement

# Boulangerie-Pâtisserie Bazin Jacques

85 BIS, RUE DE CHARENTON, 12ᵀᴴ ARR.

Telephone ✦ 01 43 07 75 21

Métro ✦ LEDRU-ROLLIN

Open FRIDAY through TUESDAY 7AM to 8PM

Closed WEDNESDAY and THURSDAY

THIS PICTURE-PERFECT NEIGHBORHOOD SHOP IS ALWAYS BUSTLING. LOCALS FROM THIS BUSY *QUARTIER* NEAR THE marché d'Aligre, one of Paris most colorful food markets, file in and out buying croissants, *madeleines*, baguettes, and sandwiches.

Fresh fruit tarts are baked on large sheets and cut into squares bubbling with apricot, rhubarb, or apple and pistachio cream. The *viennoiserie* are tasty, if a bit too buttery for my taste. *Pâtisseries* are an afterthought—they are nothing special, with the usual selection of classics like the *Paris-Brest*, *baba au rhum*, *meringue*, and *délice*. The *chou caramel* is particularly good.

Set on one corner of a quiet convergence of side streets, with a lovely old façade and a 1906 pale pink and green floral mosaic interior, this is a neighborhood classic. Friendly and efficient service manages the steady stream of customers, keeping the line moving quickly.

# Les Noces d'Or

17, RUE D'ALIGRE, 12TH ARR.

Telephone ✦ 01 43 43 18 22

Métro ✦ LEDRU-ROLLIN

Open TUESDAY through SUNDAY 9AM to 8PM

Closed MONDAY (EXCEPT during RAMADAN)

THIS TINY BAKERY SPECIALIZES IN AUTHENTIC ALGERIAN AND TUNISIAN SWEETS. LARGE ROUND PANS OF GOOEY *kalbelouz* (which means "heart of the almond"), a syrup-soaked almond and semolina cake, are stacked behind the door, ready for sale. At the counter, plates are piled with squiggly almond pistachio twists and pastry twirled into "sacks" of honey and almond paste. None of the pastries are labeled, leaving those unfamiliar with the sweets to guess about the contents, but shopkeepers and clients alike are happy to answer questions or point out their favorites.

Although not sweet, the shop specialty is the *crêpe froment* filled with sweet red pepper, *piment*, and onions. The *pain maison*, white bread sold in large fluffy wedges, is a tasty change of pace from the baguette.

# La Ruche à Miel

19, RUE D'ALIGRE, 12TH ARR.

Telephone ✦ 01 43 41 27 10

Métro ✦ LEDRU-ROLLIN

Open TUESDAY through SUNDAY 9AM to 7:30PM ✦ Closed MONDAY

SOME SAY THIS *SALON DE THÉ* SERVES PARIS' BEST ALGERIAN MINT TEA. THE PASTRIES ARE PRETTY GOOD TOO, MAKING this a nice spot to sample both on a cool day. Try the date or almond *toile de lune*, the pistachio almond or caramel nut *skandrietta*, or the cinnamon orange zest nut *cigars*, to name a few. Honey-soaked *zlabia* (fried dough) sits in pots next to the register, dripping with sugar. Homemade breads made from traditional Maghreb recipes include fluffy white wheels of *matlou*. A lunch menu offers traditional savory couscous specialties.

# THIRTEENTH
*Arrondissement*

# Laurent Duchene

2, RUE WURTZ, 13TH ARR.

*Telephone* ◆ 01 45 65 00 77

*Métro* ◆ GLACIÈRE

*Open* MONDAY *through* SATURDAY 7:30AM *to* 8PM

UCHENE'S SUCCESS AND REPUTE DESPITE HIS SHOP'S OUT-OF-THE-WAY LOCATION IN THE THIRTEENTH TESTIFIES TO just how talented he is. His pastries are a *merveille*, attracting attention from all over Paris. He balances classics like a *tarte aux*

*pommes* piled high with caramelized apples with the extraordinary, such as the *equinox*, a coriander ganache with lime zest chocolate mousse. Raspberry chocolate cake or pastry with passion fruit and chocolate cream are a few other eye-catching options.

*"Les goûters,"* or snack cakes geared for the after school crowd, include orange, apple caramel, or almond. Delicious *financiers* and *noisette* cookies in coffee or chocolate can also satisfy an adult appetite.

Duchene's beautiful yellow-and-blue-tiled shop is a classic neighborhood *pâtisserie*, quintessentially Parisian, and definitely worth a stop.

# FIFTEENTH

*Arrondissement*

# Le Moulin de la Vièrge

166, AVENUE DE SUFFREN, 15TH ARR.

Telephone ◆ 01 47 83 45 55

Métro ◆ SÉGUR

Open MONDAY through SATURDAY 7AM to 8PM ◆ Closed SUNDAY

---

THIS DEPENDABLE CHAIN OFFERS HIGH-QUALITY BREADS, *VIENNOISERIE*, AND A FEW PASTRIES. THE SWEET BREADS like the *cannelé bordelais*, the bite-sized chewy specialty from Bordeaux, are always fresh and delicious. The *financier* is particularly good. Try the specialty *carré Dijonnais*, a *sablé* smothered with blackberry preserves, or the *carré au miel*, coated in nuts and honey.

---

### ◆ ◆ ◆ Additional Locations ◆ ◆ ◆

105 RUE VERCINGÉTORIX, 14TH ARR.

Telephone 01 45 43 09 84 ◆ Métro PERNETY or PLAISANCE

Open MONDAY through SATURDAY 7:30AM to 8PM ◆ Closed SUNDAY

◆

82 RUE DAGUERRE, 14TH ARR.

Telephone 01 43 22 50 55 ◆ Métro GAITÉ

Open MONDAY through SATURDAY 7:30AM to 8PM ◆ Closed SUNDAY

◆

6 RUE DE LEVIS, 17TH ARR.

Telephone 01 43 87 42 42 ◆ Métro VILLIERS or MALESHERBES

Open THURSDAY through TUESDAY 7:30AM to 8PM ◆ Closed WEDNESDAY

---

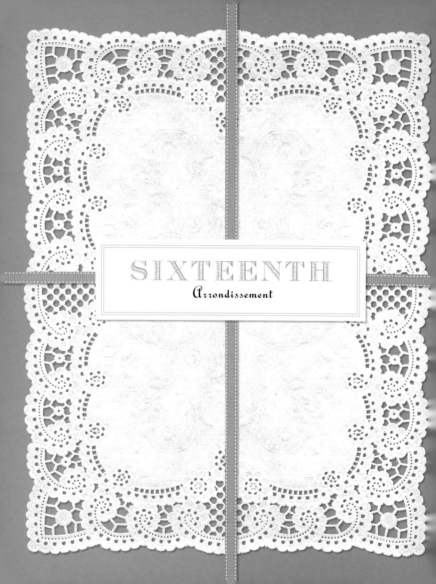

# SIXTEENTH

*Arrondissement*

# Béchu

118, AVENUE VICTOR HUGO, 16ᵀᴴ ARR.

*Telephone* ✦ 01 47 27 97 79

*Métro* ✦ VICTOR HUGO

*Open* TUESDAY *through* SUNDAY 7AM *to* 8:30PM

ÉCHU'S PLEASANT *SALON DE THÉ* AND ABUNDANCE OF OUT-DOOR SIDEWALK TABLES MAKES IT A PERFECT SPOT FOR an afternoon snack. The specialty *feuillantine* is a chocolate praline lover's dream. Also good are the *Trocadero*, a vanilla meringue pastry, or its chocolate sibling, the *Victor Hugo*.

# Boissier

184, AVENUE VICTOR HUGO, 16TH ARR.

Telephone ✦ 01 45 03 50 77

Métro ✦ VICTOR HUGO

Open MONDAY through SATURDAY 9AM to 7PM

THIS CHOCOLATE SHOP IS FAMOUS FOR ITS SPECIALTY *PÉTALES*, DELICATELY SCULPTED CHOCOLATE PETALS FLAVORED WITH fruit or flower essences. Beautifully packaged with a multi-colored mix of strawberry, lime, or clementine, or *verveine* and rose, among others, they make a lovely gift.

Less refined are the gooey chocolate *confitures*, fruit and chocolate spreads. For slathering on toast or crêpes or eating by the spoonful, try chocolate banana, raspberry, or orange varieties. My favorite is the white chocolate mango.

Don't look for non-chocolate goods *chez* Boissier—you'll only find a limited selection of cakes and caramels.

# Carette

4, PLACE DU TROCADÉRO, 16TH ARR.

Telephone ✦ 01 47 27 88 56 85

Métro ✦ TROCADÉRO

Open DAILY 7AM to 11:30PM

"MAIS CARETTE, BIEN SÛR," RESPONDS ANY LOCAL WHEN ASKED FOR A BONNE ADDRESSE NEAR THE TROCADÉRO. Who would guess such a delicious *Parisien* spot could exist at the heart of one of the most touristy parts of the city? Carette is a lovely *salon de thé*, with a menu of excellent quality *pâtisseries*, homemade ice cream, made-to-order crêpes, and light lunch options like salads and fancy sandwiches.

House specialties include hot chocolate, *millefeuille*, and *macarons*, but my favorites are the *verrines*, a parfait of vanilla cream, fig compote, fresh raspberries, and pistachio cream, and the *Catalane*, a shortbread tart of rhubarb compote, fresh strawberries, and vanilla cream. On a warm day, try the *coupe Carette*, vanilla and praline ice cream with

"grandmother's" chocolate mousse smothered in chocolate sauce with whipped cream.

Carette's food is top-notch, but its primary appeal is its location on the place du Trocadéro. The wide terrace doesn't have a view of the Eiffel Tower, but it does have plenty of tables for people watching. Service is friendly and welcoming and the full menu is served all day.

# Carton

150, AVENUE VICTOR HUGO, 16TH ARR.

Telephone ✦ 01 47 04 66 55

Métro ✦ VICTOR HUGO or RUE DE LA POMPE

Open OPENING HOURS

IT WAS THE *PAVÉ CITRON* THAT FIRST BROUGHT CARTON TO MY ATTENTION. I DEVOURED THE BRIOCHE LEMON CURD "sandwich" within seconds when I first discovered it in this nondescript, modern-looking *pâtisserie* in the sixteenth arrondissement.

In subsequent visits, I could hardly tear myself away from the *pavé citron*, but eventually I branched out and tried specialties, as recommended by Madame Carton herself, the *chocolat feuilleté* and the *millefeuille aux framboises.*

Monsieur and Madame Carton opened their first Paris *pâtisserie* in 1978, quickly expanded, and now the two shops are under separate management. The sixteenth arrondissement shop has a pleasant *salon de thé,* convenient for a quick pastry and coffee break or a light lunch of quiche, tarts, salads, or omelets. Lunch is served from noon to 4 p.m. Pastries and savory snacks (quiches, pizzas, etc.) are available at the counter all day.

### ✦ ✦ ✦ Additional Location ✦ ✦ ✦

6, RUE DE BUCI, 6TH ARR.

Telephone 01 43 26 04 13 ✦ Métro MABILLON

Open MONDAY through SATURDAY 7AM to 8PM ✦ Closed MONDAY

# Mazet

116, AVENUE VICTOR HUGO, 16TH ARR.

*Telephone* ✦ 01 44 05 18 08

*Métro* ✦ VICTOR HUGO

OPEN MONDAY through FRIDAY 10AM to 7PM

*Closed* SATURDAY and SUNDAY

THIS CENTURY-OLD, FAMILY-RUN *CHOCOLATIER* HAS MADE ITS NAME IN PRALINES. *PRALINES MAZET DE MONTARGIS* are based on an original recipe for roasted and caramelized almonds created 350 years ago during Louis XIII's reign. While faithful to the original praline, Mazet has expanded the line, adding specialties like *givrettes* and *grelons*, caramelized almonds and hazelnuts, respectively, wrapped in milk chocolate with a dab of caramel. To coat the *nougatine* evenly in dark chocolate, Mazet uses the old-fashioned method—spinning them in an open cauldron for hours at a time while hand-pouring chocolate over them. The *chocolatier*'s ear tells him when to pour in fresh liquid chocolate—the candies start to make a harder "clinking" noise against the pot when they're ready for another coat. After six to seven hours of continuous spinning and pouring, the process yields 350 kilograms of identically formed—and delicious!—chocolate-covered candies.

# Pascal le Glacier

17, RUE BOIS-LE-VENT, 16TH ARR.

*Telephone* ✦ 01 45 27 61 84

*Métro* ✦ LA MUETTE

*Open* TUESDAY *through* SATURDAY 10:30AM *to* 7PM

*Closed* SUNDAY *and* MONDAY

PASCAL LE GLACIER HAS BEEN A FAVORITE SIXTEENTH ARR-ONDISSEMENT ICE CREAM STOP FOR MORE THAN TWENTY-three years, serving up seasonal flavors like rhubarb, apricot, and strawberry, and year-round choices such as chocolate cinnamon, caramel ginger, licorice, and of course, all the classics.

This not-so-charming storefront is more geared to takeaway tubs of the creamy treat, but cones are available. You can also find Pascal's ice cream at Café de Flore, the landmark café in the sixth arrondissement, and in a few top Paris restaurants.

# Yamazaki Pâtisserie-Salon de Thé

6, CHAUSSÉE DE LA MUETTE, 16TH ARR.

Téléphone ◆ 01 40 50 19 19

Métro ◆ LA MUETTE

Open DAILY 9AM to 7PM

IN THIS *VIEILLE FRANCE QUARTIER* FILLED WITH OLD FAMILIES WITH DISCRIMINATING AND DEMANDING PALATES, Yamazuki's superb cakes have a reputation as among the best. The *pralinette*, a layered pastry of praline, almond, and hazelnut mousse and meringue biscuits, is a neighborhood favorite. The *trois chocolat*, a luscious mound of creamy white, milk, and dark chocolate mousse, is not to be mistaken for the *Tahiti*, a similarly formed, equally delicious concoction of *crème brulée*, *crème vanille*, and *bavarois chocolat guanaja*. The curd in the ample lemon tart is velvety smooth and deliciously tangy. Traditional Japanese cakes, a nod to Yamazuki's Japanese heritage (it is owned by a Japanese company), are an unusual treat, with two spongy layers sandwiching a filling of sweet bean paste.

In contrast to the pastries, the shop is unimpressive and uninspiring, although conveniently offers a *salon de thé* for enjoying sweets or the excellent quiches *sur place*.

# SEVENTEENTH

*Arrondissement*

# Charpentier Chocolatier

87, RUE DE COURCELLES, 17TH ARR.

Telephone ✦ 01 47 63 93 05

Métro ✦ COURCELLES

Open MONDAY through SATURDAY 9AM to 7PM ✦ Closed SUNDAY

CHARPENTIER HAS SUPPLIED THIS QUIET, RESIDENTIAL NEIGHBORHOOD NEAR PARC MONCEAU WITH SOME OF PARIS' best artisanal chocolates for over fifty years. Employees have been there almost as long as the shop, offering sample morsels and descriptions of specialties like *la rivoirine*, a marzipan treat with rum-soaked raisins and milk chocolate bits, coated in powdered sugar, and available in cookie or bite-sized candy forms. Chocolate *macarons* filled with creamy ganache are also a neighborhood favorite. I like the classic praline chocolates, but original tastes like licorice or lemon zest are fun too.

# L'Écureuil

96, RUE DE LEVIS, 17TH ARR.

*Telephone* ✦ 01 42 27 28 27

*Métro* ✦ VILLIERS or MALESHERBES

*Open* TUESDAY *through* SATURDAY 9AM to 8PM

THIS SPARKLING NEWLY-OPENED *PÂTISSERIE* IS BASED ON A CONCEPT OF HIGHEST-QUALITY INGREDIENTS—FRESH FRUIT from the market, butter churned every morning the old-fashioned way, fresh whole Alsatian milk. L'Écureuil's tarts and pastries certainly reveal the quality, though they're not discernibly better than those from other *pâtisseries* that make the "highest quality" claim. The *kara*, a caramel and praline cream-filled mound with a thin layer of *feuillitine*, is a success, but the specialty *Beaumont*, two *dacquoise* chocolate biscuits sandwiching Calvados-simmered apples and vanilla ginger cream is unexciting. The description leaves one craving more as both the Calvados and ginger flavors are hardly detectable. Orange or pistachio cakes are moist and soft in the center, but the *madeleines* are a bit dry for my taste.

Nonetheless, this *pâtisserie* is a fun, punchy addition to the neighborhood with an eye-catching atmosphere that begs you to try its chocolates, jams, and design-conscious packages of biscuits as well as its *pâtisseries*. The icing on the cake is the shop's pledge to respect the environment with its packaging and limited waste.

# EIGHTEENTH

*Arrondissement*

# Arnaud Larher

53, RUE CAULAINCOURT, 18TH ARR.

Telephone ✦ 01 42 57 68 08

Métro ✦ LAMARCK-CAULAINCOURT

Open TUESDAY through SATURDAY 10AM to 7:30PM

PRALINE CHOCOLATE FANS SHOULDN'T MISS *CHOCOLATIER* ARNAUD LARHER'S GANACHE *PRALINÉ* AND *PISTACHE praliné* (called the *jade*), melt-in-your-mouth delicacies that swept first and second prizes in their category at Paris' *Salon de Chocolat*, the "see and be seen" chocolate show held every November.

Larher's chocolates are revered for their purity and delicacy, and his pastries are prizeworthy too. *Macarons* come in a bursting cherry and pistachio combination, a more subtle violet or a powerfully caffeinated coffee, to name a few. Specialty pastries include a classic *Saint-Honoré* in vanilla or caramel and a *savarin au vieux rhum* with whipped cream. The *millefeuille du moment* surprises with varieties like orange, raspberry, or strawberry and the *baba du jour* shocks with tropical fruit rather than the traditional rum.

Chocolate creations being Larher's *coup de coeur*, be sure to try the *moelleux au chocolat*, a rich muffin-size cake with a molten center, or the *Toulouse Lautrec*, chocolate cake layered with dark chocolate *crème brulée* and bitter chocolate mousse.

Interestingly, Larher is one of the few French *chocolatiers* who pays any attention to milk chocolate. While most are dismissive of anything but extra-dark cocoa, Larher features a solid milk chocolate bar and a house specialty ganache of smooth creamy milk chocolate.

# NINETEENTH
## Arrondissement

# La Boulangerie par Véronique Mauclerc

83, RUE DE CRIMÉE, 19TH ARR.

Telephone ✦ 01 42 40 64 55

Métro ✦ LAUMIÈRE

Open THURSDAY through MONDAY 8AM to 8PM

Closed TUESDAY and WEDNESDAY

ARTISAN *BOULANGÈRE* VÉRONIQUE MAUCLERC BAKES HER BREADS IN THIS *BOULANGERIE*'S ORIGINAL WOOD-FIRED oven, dating from 1902, one of two remaining in Paris. The oven gives the bread a golden crust, a moist center, and deep flavor. The *pain pistaches, amandes, et noisettes* (pistachio, almond, and hazelnut bread) is a neighborhood favorite. The *pain aux cereales* and other whole grain varieties are also good.

Mauclerc is an artisanal *pâtissière* as well as *boulangère*, but purists beware: The distinctive wood-fired taste that makes the bread so good can be a bit off-putting in pastries. Sometimes it works well, rendering the classic *tarte au citron* an unusual, yet interesting, texture and taste. The *fondant chocolat* and the *royale* are also successful. But the oven's hard-to-control temperature and high heat can leave pastries well-done and uneven in quality.

This *boulangerie* is worth a stop if only to see its circa-1930s original lilac-tiled walls and ceiling fresco by Italian painter Panzani. There is also a cozy *salon de thé* in the back with a view of the oven. The brunch special offers juice, coffee, a choice of *viennoiserie* and fruit tart, and fresh bread with butter and jams *"à volonté"* (all you can eat). The *salon de thé* serves any time during the *boulangerie*'s open hours.

In nice weather, picnic in nearby Buttes Chaumont park and enjoy the neighborhood scene. Modeled after New York's Central Park, it's one of Paris' most original.

# TWENTIETH
### Arrondissement

# Ice to Ice Gelateria Café

30–32, BOULEVARD DE MÉNILMONTANT, 20TH ARR.

Telephone ✦ 01 43 58 44 16

Métro ✦ PÈRE LACHAISE

Open DAILY 10AM to 11PM

THIS *GELATERIA*/CAFÉ ON THE CORNER OF BUSY PLACE AUGUSTE MÉTIVIER, AT THE ENTRANCE OF PÈRE LACHAISE cemetery, is perfectly placed for a cone before paying respects to Paris' illustrious dead. Ice to Ice's heaping cones of Italian-style *gelato* come in fun flavors like cookies and *tiramisu*. The more than twenty house-made daily flavors get my vote for creamiest ice cream in Paris. *En plus*, prices start at 1.50 euros for a *tout petit cornet*, one of Paris's cheapest, quality cones. Ice to Ice also serves Italian coffee, fresh fruit juices, light sandwiches, and homemade waffles.

# The Galette des Rois

THE NEW YEAR IN FRANCE ALSO STARTS THE SEASON OF THE *GALETTE DES ROIS*, THE CELEBRATION OF THE EPIPHANY CENTERED AROUND EATING THIS *FEUILTAGE* PASTRY FILLED WITH FRANGIPANE CREAM. THE ACTUAL CHRISTIAN FEAST DAY IS JANUARY 6, BUT THE CAKES ARE SOLD AND ENJOYED THROUGHOUT THE FIRST THREE WEEKS IN JANUARY. ACCORDING TO FRENCH TRADITION, FAMILIES CONGREGATE ON THE SECOND SUNDAY AFTER CHRISTMAS TO SHARE THE *GALETTE* AND CELEBRATE THE FEAST. A *FÈVE* (ORIGINALLY A BEAN, BUT NOW USUALLY A PLASTIC TRINKET), IS HIDDEN INSIDE THE CAKE, AND WHOEVER GETS THE WEDGE WITH THE *FÈVE* IS "CROWNED" AND IS RESPONSIBLE FOR BUYING THE NEXT CAKE.

As soon as the New Year is heralded, *galettes* become a topic of hot competition among *pâtisseries*, each trying to outdo by inventing exotic varieties and/or perfecting the classic recipe. The *galettes* are big business, with some shops even adding Sunday hours to supply cakes to neighborhood patrons. Purists claim the traditional recipe best, with a flaky, not too greasy *feuilté* crust and a frangipane filling (a mixture of one-third *crème pâtissière* and two-thirds *crème d'amande*), that is not too thick or sweet.

Recipes vary by region, with some using almond instead of frangipane cream or a brioche dough rather than *feuiltage*.

# The Éclair: France's Favorite Pâtisserie

MOST ANY *PÂTISSERIE* OWNER WILL CONFIRM— THE ÉCLAIR HOLDS THE TITLE OF THE FRENCH'S FAVORITE PASTRY. IT'S HARD TO IDENTIFY PRECISELY THIS BEST-SELLER'S UNIVERSAL APPEAL, BUT ONE CAN GUESS THAT IT'S BECAUSE IT'S UNFUSSY, RELATIVELY EASY TO EAT, NOT TOO RICH, AND EXTREMELY SATISFYING FOR A SWEET BITE. A SIMPLE COMBINATION OF *CHOU* PASTRY WITH *CRÈME PÂTISSIÈRE* FILLING AND A GLAZED TOP, THIS OBLONG PASTRY IS EATEN AT ANY TIME OF THE DAY AND CAN BE GOBBLED ON THE GO.

"The best" éclair is a topic of great debate, but most fans agree that certain attributes are necessary. First, the *pâte à chou* shell should be soft and fresh, with no hint of crustiness or staleness. Second, the cream interior must be classic *crème pâtissière*, light and luscious on the tongue. Icing should be smooth and evenly coated. In the case of a chocolate éclair (the preferred variety), real chocolate should always be used, never powder. The shape is important too—it shouldn't be too big (unwieldy to eat) or too small (unsatisfying to bite).

Beyond these criteria, there is little agreement, and pastry chefs take liberties with the formula to create innovative variations like green tea, pistachio, and multicolored fruit flavors.

Éclair means "lightning" or "flash" in French and some say this pastry got its name from the speed with which it is devoured. Others suggest that the name comes from the glossy shine of the icing topping.

Several other classic pastries take their cue from the éclair, offering up similar ingredient combinations in different forms—the *religieuse* or the Paris-Brest, for example—but none occupy the same place in Parisian hearts or pastry counters.

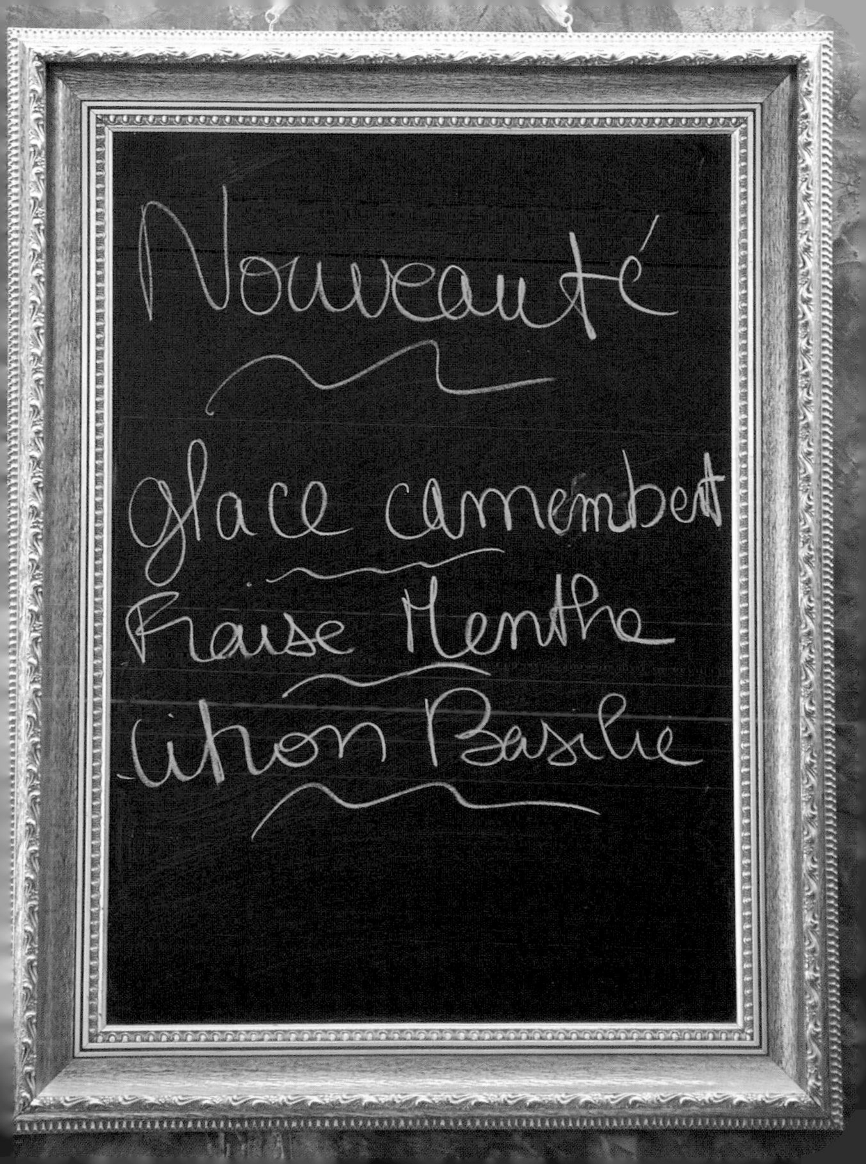
Nouveauté
Glace camembert
Fraise Menthe
Citron Basilic

# INDEX

# INDEX

## BY BUSINESS TYPE

## Chocolatiers and Confiseries

## Good For Gifts

# About the Author

JAMIE CAHILL WORKED IN JOURNALISM, public relations, and marketing before moving to Paris and focusing on writing. She is a lifelong dessert lover and recently completed the city of Paris' professional *pâtisserie* course. She now lives in London.

# About the Photographer

ALISON HARRIS IS BASED IN PARIS. Her photographs have illustrated cookbooks, advertising campaigns, magazine stories, and books, including *Markets of Paris* (The Little Bookroom). Her work can be seen at www.alisonharris.com